DON'T STOP NOW

Finding Purpose and Passion in
Your Career and Personal Journey

Don't Stop Now

FINDING PURPOSE AND PASSION IN YOUR CAREER AND PERSONAL JOURNEY

DR. CHARLES REDD

StoryTerrace

Text Diana Holquist, on behalf of Story Terrace

Design Grade Design and Adeline Media

Copyright © Dr. Charles Redd

First print October 2019

StoryTerrace

www.StoryTerrace.com

CONTENTS

INTRODUCTION   9

PART I: The Four Keys to Discovering and
        Living Your Purpose

1. IF NOT NOW, WHEN?   15
   Finding Your Purpose in Life and Career

2. NEVER GIVE UP ON YOUR DREAMS   31
   Why Grow? Why Change? Why Persevere?

3. YOU ARE A DIAMOND IN THE ROUGH.
   THERE IS NONE OTHER LIKE YOU.   45
   How to Grow Into Your Purpose—Step 1: Education

4. LIFE IS ABOUT SETTING AND
   ACHIEVING GOALS   57
   How to Achieve Your Purpose—Step 2: Making a Plan and
   Sticking to It

5. LIFE'S TWISTS AND TURNS:
   THE LEAP OF FAITH   69
   How to Achieve Your Purpose—Step 3: The Leap
   of Faith

6. STAYING FOCUSED IS THE KEY   83
How to Achieve Your Purpose—Step 4: The Secret
of Perseverance

7. DELAYED BUT NOT DENIED   97
External Roadblocks and How to Overcome Them

8. DON'T BE YOUR OWN
WORST ENEMY   111
Learn and Grow from Your Mistakes

PART II: You Changed Yourself, Now Change
the World

9. WHAT GOT US HERE WON'T GET
US THERE   125
Why Leadership Matters for Everyone. Yes, Even You!

10. MY TIME, MY TURN   141
The Link Between Personal Growth and Leadership

11. PUTTING YOUR BEST FOOT
FORWARD   155
Different Kinds of Leaders and the Importance
of Teamwork

12. FROM MOUNTAINTOP TO
    MOUNTAINTOP   169
    Passing the Mantle: The True Meaning of Leadership and
    of Your Life

CONCLUSION   179

ABOUT THE AUTHOR   185

INTRODUCTION

People say to me, *Dr. Charles, you live comfortably. You have a solid career. A loving family. A strong faith. You're happy. So what do you mean, don't stop now? Why on earth would you want to change anything about your life? Why not STOP? Relax in your success? Enjoy what you have?*

I could answer these questions with the typical reasons a person might want to change their life:

- Times are changing. It used to be, you stayed at one company, one job. You'd reach 55, 62, then retire to enjoy a quiet life. All around me, I see people who still attempt to live this way. But this, in my opinion, is no longer our world.
- Technology is eliminating jobs; we must change to keep up.
- People are living longer, outliving their savings. Slowing down is no longer an option.
- People become bored without new challenges.
- People fear they'll become lonely if they don't expand their social networks.
- People fear their minds and bodies will become weak if not constantly stimulated and challenged.

These are all excellent reasons to keep moving forward. But none of these are the real reason you and I must keep changing and growing. Go ahead, start with these reasons, if you like. But if you pursue change for these reasons alone, then you will not succeed.

If you pursue growth for the wrong reasons,
you will fail.

Why? Because you will be missing the most important part, the purpose of this book, and the purpose of my life and of your life, too, even if you don't know it yet.

- Believe it or not, you must change, because you are called to change. That is, you have a dream.
- You have a purpose on this earth. That is, you have a passion.
- Your purpose and passion give your life meaning, and you must not stop until you discover and fulfill this meaning.

You might believe that your purpose is God-given. Or maybe you believe that your purpose comes from inside yourself, your psychological makeup. Maybe it comes from a duty to an ethical or moral system, or it's some form of destiny, whatever that means to you.

Or, maybe you have no idea what makes you know that things aren't quite right with you and your life. But if you're honest with yourself, then you feel that tug, that urge to keep moving forward, to do something more.

You have a purpose, your life has meaning, and if you don't strive to fulfill that purpose and meaning, then you will be filled with regret.

Close your eyes. Do you see, feel, and sense a vision of yourself that does not align with your current life? That means it's time to grow; it's time to change.

This book is about how to find your purpose and how to find meaning in your life as you move along your personal journey. It's about how to listen to what God and the world are telling you, and how to answer that call.

It's not easy. It's not safe. It's not quick. But you can do it. You have the power to grow and change into the person you've always wanted to be. You have the power to have the career you've always wanted to have, no matter where you are on life's journey.

Never, never, ever give up.

How do I know you can do this? Because I did it, and I'm not anyone special. I had hardships, just like you have. I had a failed marriage, ending in divorce after 23 years. At various times in my career, I went through struggles that were unavoidable and out of my control: a reduction in sales force, a change of company management, or just plain ignorance and intolerance. And, of course, there were times when there was no fault, no reason, there was just a bad fit, something not right that I felt and knew. But I never, ever let any of that stop me. I vowed to continue to grow and change, whatever the challenge.

Be better, not bitter.

This is my story. This is how I learned what it takes to keep moving forward. This is the secret to finding purpose, failing forward, and to living a happy and fulfilling life and having a happy and fulfilling career.

Oh—and one more thing. Once you find your passion and your purpose, you must help others to find theirs, too. But we'll get to the reasons for that later. First things first. Let's get started on you.

PART I:

THE FOUR KEYS TO DISCOVERING AND LIVING YOUR PURPOSE

1

IF NOT NOW, WHEN?

Finding Your Purpose
in Life and Career

There are two great days in a person's life:
the day we were born and the day we discover why.
—*William Barclay, theologian*

The Basement Ministry

I started teaching in the basement of my grandmother's house in Detroit when I was nine years old. I saved up my allowance until I had the funds to buy enough candy to tempt my "students" to show up. It was the summer of 1966, so I only needed a few pennies to buy chocolates, gum, whatever I thought would make them come. Sheila, Anita, a few others. I remember them all to this day.

The basement was one of those wood-walled, cabin-tree-trunk

affairs. It had deer heads mounted on the walls that always scared me to death with their black, empty, staring eyes. But I was on a mission. I had a job to do.

It didn't matter to me what I taught, only that I felt compelled to teach. At the time, I lived with my grandmother and my aunt, who was a teacher in the local school, so I'd often look to her for material. She had pictures of instruments on cards, for example, so one day, I borrowed them. I showed the pictures to the other kids: violin, trumpet, French horn. It felt important and necessary. Occasionally, my grandmother would peek through the door to check on us, but we were good, serious kids. We didn't make trouble.

If I didn't have material to teach, I could always fall back on my imagination. Basement chairs would be covered with blankets to become a train, and I was the conductor. That felt like teaching too, although at the time, I didn't understand why. In any case, it didn't matter what we did. It was, even then, about community, gathering, and celebration.

Yes, always celebration. That's the part a lot of people forget.

After the lessons learned in my grandmother's basement, I would hand out the candy for my friends to grab. I was so excited to see them grabbing those candy bars. I'd taught them something and made them smile. I'd created a community. I'd brought us together. I was play-acting my purpose as a kid, but even then, the desire was there, the dream: I was forming my first ministry. This would eventually become the meaning and the purpose of my own life.

I pursued my basement ministry with the zeal, innocence, and optimism that only a child can possess. It was play, but I was learning the skills and truths that would become the bedrock of my future life. One day, I recall Billy Smith, the preacher's kid, and Toby Ellis, who could sing, decided to play church. I couldn't preach back then to save my own life, much less anyone else's. I couldn't sing a lick, but I was able to bring people together. I could yield to them, give them space and the use of my operation, my vision, my candy supply, and my grandmother's basement, antlers and all.

We turned down the lights and got down on our knees. Billy preached. Toby sang. We all prayed. It was almost too much to take in, too powerful to put into words. Sure, some of the kids had shown up for the chocolate, but they always left with something more. And I had learned the first priceless lesson that would change my life:

To lead often means to step aside and let others shine.

Everyone had a role. Everyone had a purpose. Mine was to bring those talents together, to be the conductor of the orchestra, or the blanket-and-chair train, or whatever we were up to that day. We'd raise our voices to the sky and let the Spirit shine through us.

My whole life was there, already defined, in my grandmother's basement. It would take me most of my adult life to rediscover it, because the minute I "grew up," I abandoned my purpose. Of course, I did—don't we all? We're told to be practical, to be prudent, to put our dreams away for career, for money, for survival, for the desires of others.

First, while in college during the summer for two consecutive years, I worked at the Ford Motor Company. I worked twelve-hour shifts, from five in the morning to five in the afternoon. Then I would immediately head to work for a second job at the Rouge Golf driving range, working from 6 p.m. to 10:30 p.m. I can remember working in the Ford foundry plant. It was 100 degrees and more. I had to wear white masks over my nose to protect my lungs. Then, the other two summers while in college, it was Sears, Roebuck & Company as a salesman in the men's department, then in a bank as a teller.

I was successful, happy, and on my way to… well… somewhere.

I didn't bother to ask myself where.

Once I was out of college (yes, all those jobs were before I'd even graduated college; that's how soon we abandon our true purposes in life), I started my career after graduation at General Foods as a sales representative for the Maxwell House Coffee Division. Soon, I was climbing the corporate ladder at Pepsi-Cola, Coca-Cola, Faygo Beverages, Frito-Lay, and The Hershey Company.

I looked like a person who had it going on. I looked like a person who was on their way. And I was. I was thriving, learning, leading, and I loved it. I still do.

But something was missing. Something just didn't feel right. The call of my grandmother's basement was always with me.

One excellent way to discover your purpose is to think back to your childhood. What did you always love since the very beginning?
What did you do before you started doing what the adult world said you should do? What are your fondest memories from the past?

I was 26 years old when I decided to heed the call. I would take the leap of faith—more on that important concept later—and dedicate my life to teaching and leading in the corporate world, in the field of education for higher learning, and in the spiritual world through discipleship.

It's never, ever too late to find and follow your purpose in life.

Knowing is Nothing Without Doing

All those years I spent climbing the corporate ladder weren't wasted. They were preparation—again, more on that later. But there is always the risk that we'll take all this preparation to find and follow our true purpose, then fail to act.

- We must prepare: once we find our purpose, it'll take work. So we must get started as soon as we can.
- We must dare: once we find our purpose, it'll take a leap of faith. So we must be willing to act.

- We must be aware: once we find our purpose, we must keep it always in our sights, even when it seems too far away to matter. Our purpose must be our guiding star.

Everyone has a purpose in life.
Our first purpose is to find our purpose.

What is Purpose?

Purpose is passion. It is that thing that you just can't stop doing, even if it makes no sense. It is something within that drives you. Listen to that voice inside you. When I finally found and accepted my purpose, my life changed forever. I was able to stop using my time, talents, and energy going down paths that weren't the right path. Once I found the right path, I said to myself, "I will die empty." That is leaving a positive legacy that inspires and touches people lives. I plan to just blaze away on fire versus wilting away in some corner.

The Origins of Purpose: Is It Given by God?

This is not a book about religion, and yet, without religion, what does it mean to have purpose? If we say that we are put on this earth for a purpose, then who put us here? Who gave us this purpose? Is it possible to have a purpose in life if one doesn't believe in an active and loving God?

Yes. Absolutely.

As a minister, of course I believe in God. I've been saved, and I preach the love of God to anyone who will listen—and even to quite a few who won't. When I act based on my purpose, I say that I am following God's directive. For example:

- I left my ministry training, then came back years later, because I was compelled to come back. An inner voice (I believe the Holy Spirit) spoke to me. I couldn't help myself but to come back. This, to me, is an indicator of being led by God.

- Often in my life, a person's name comes to mind—*Dr. Charles, you need to call so-and-so.* (It could be anyone, but for the purposes of this example, let's say "Johnny Doe.") I don't know why I must do this; I just feel compelled. So I call, and when I do, Johnny says, "I really wanted to talk to you. How'd you know?" I knew because I was led by God.

- In the spring of 2017, my mother was in assisted living. I felt compelled to fly to Detroit for her birthday and again for Mother's Day to see her. I said to her on my last visit, "Let's take a selfie." After, in the hallway as I left her room, the tears came. Something in my spirit didn't say "last time," but it sure felt like it. I had known I had better get there to see her. My mother passed away in the summer that year. That day in May was the last time we were together. I went to Detroit because I was led by God.

I know plenty of people who don't believe in God the way I do. They hear these stories of mine and say that I had been following my heart. Or my sixth sense. These people might say, *I had a gut feeling.* That's fine. It doesn't matter how you interpret the pull that something has on you. What is important is that you act on it. There are a lot of ways to interpret purpose in this world:

- **Passion:** Many people equate their purpose on Earth with their passion. This person would say, *Dr. Charles, you came back to the ministry, because it was your passion. It was what you loved to do, and this is why you couldn't live without it.* In other words, I was led by my desire. If you see your purpose as the same as your passion, then you are this sort of person. People who lead their lives guided by passion are some of the most successful people we know, because these people do what they love with no apologies and no regrets.

Don't ask yourself what the world needs; ask yourself what makes you come alive. And then go and do that. Because what the world needs is more people who have come alive.

—Howard Thurman

- **Destiny:** Many people who don't believe in God still believe that they have a destiny; that is, that they have a purpose on this earth that is dictated by the universe. This can mean many things to many people, but the core of this belief is that there is something outside us, operating on us, that we feel deep down. These people would say, *Dr. Charles, you felt the urge to call Johnny Doe, because on some level, you are connected with him.* These interconnections, the pull of humanity and of nature, are powerful ones. These people don't need a God to know there is something out there that they don't understand. They still know that to lead a truly fulfilling life, they must acknowledge and respect this pull.

Destiny is the push of our instincts to the pull of our purpose.
—T.D. Jakes

- **Ethics, Morals, and The Golden Rule:** We used to wear wristbands that said, "WWJD?"—"What Would Jesus Do?" Another way of putting this is: do unto others as you would have them do unto you. The Golden Rule is to respect and to love others. It maps out a way of being in the world, a way to act. It's based on scripture, but it's also about ethics or morals. You act on a code of respect and kindness, because it feels right to you. Thus, you're pulled to do the right thing by your moral code. When you believe in a moral code, your purpose comes from a common humanity, a calling each person has inside of them to act in a way that brings the greatest human good. You are acting in life based on natural law and rationality. This is a powerful way to define purpose: I am called to this thing in the world based on my belief that as moral beings, we must fulfill our purpose as defined by our common humanity, our responsibilities to one another as human beings.
- **Experience:** We all form opinions and decide how to act depending on what we've learned in the past. When we have gathered experience, we can exercise wisdom. Wisdom comes from learning from experience. Smokers can observe

other smokers who are sick or dying and feel themselves compelled to stop smoking. A person who believes his purpose comes from his wisdom or experience would say, *Dr. Charles, you went to visit your mother, because as a minister, you knew the signs of a person at the end of their life. This is why you knew that you had to go to her.* This sort of person observes life and carefully attends to it, and thus can follow their purpose based on rationality: this is what I must do, because I have seen it before, and thus know the best course of action.

There's only one thing more painful than learning from experience and that's not learning from experience.

—Archibald McLeash

No matter your reasoning—maybe you believe in all of these motivators at once; I do!—all humans know deep down that they have a specific purpose to carry out, a calling toward what they were made for. We know we have not been produced as human beings to wander around aimlessly. Believe in obedience to your purpose, for whatever reason suits you best, and you're on your way to a more meaningful and happy life.

Believing in your purpose can mean believing in God, believing in humanity, or just simply believing in yourself. Whatever your belief, respect and value it. You know deep down that there is truth in your instinct.

This is what it means to be human. This is what it means to have purpose.

The Difference Between Purpose and a Dream

A dream is a person standing on the sidewalk, looking through the windows of a department store. They see something they want: a suit, a tie, a skirt, a pair of Italian leather shoes. But a purpose is something more. You are standing outside that store and looking in, and you see yourself doing something. Your vision is of you acting, not of material things. From early on, I had a vision: I could speak and have impact and reach people and change their lives. I saw myself doing it. I would close my eyes. I was on a stage. I saw people learning. When your purpose is to sing, when you close your eyes, you see yourself on a stage wowing an audience with your songs. Dreams are a fantasy based on the end result; purpose is a life's work where the joy is in the doing.

How to Find Your Purpose: The $10 Question

I always knew what I was called to do in life. But not everyone is so lucky.

I've recruited on college campuses for Fortune 500 companies at career fairs. Imagine 150 or more companies, every company with a booth. When I recruited for The Hershey Company, I always had a huge advantage, because I had a draw no struggling student could resist: candy.

Students would come up to our booth, more interested in the chocolate than in giving me a résumé. They didn't realize they were walking into a trap.

"Hey what do you got, Hershey?" they'd ask as they dug into the bowl of silver foil-wrapped kisses.

"What is it you want?" I'd ask.

"A job," they'd say, stuffing the kisses into bags, pockets, and their mouths.

"We're not offering a job," I'd say.

That would usually stop them for a moment. Wasn't this a career fair?

Now that I had their attention, I'd go in for the jugular. "We're offering a career. You need to know what you want to do."

"I want to get paid."

"Okay. Let me ask you this: If every profession in the whole world all paid ten dollars an hour, which would you choose?"

Now they were hooked. Chances are, no one had ever spoken to them like this. They'd been told to seek high salaries, high status. They'd been told their whole lives to listen to their pocketbooks and their heads, but never to their hearts.

"Any job. Chef, teacher, park ranger, street sweeper. Or maybe a corporate leader in a candy company bringing up others in the building of a corporate culture where all can thrive and prosper. It doesn't matter what you want, just listen to your call. Therein lies a clue where your passion lies."

This message would resonate with everyone. I'd tell them, "Postmen have a spirit of the outdoors, of walking and moving. Corporate leaders have a spirit of leading. Servers have a spirit of serving. That's not a job I'd like to do, but there are those who love it. They'd rather be in a busy, bustling restaurant, kidding around with the regulars and providing joy and nourishment than in a corporate office, banging on a computer. Everyone has something to offer. Don't just wander around this place, asking what we've got. Ask yourself what you've got. Find your zone."

Usually, by the end of our talk, I'd gotten a résumé, maybe even set up an interview if I'd liked what I'd seen and heard. That was my zone: leading people, educating them, letting them know there's something more in this world that matters more than they can know when they focus on the wrong things for the wrong reasons:

- You will never fulfill your destiny doing work you despise. Sure, you can have a job to pay the bills. But having a career is something different. It's a long-term perspective. I urge you to look not just at your career, but at your life from this long-term perspective, this "career" perspective. Continue on with the passion in everything you do. As author John C. Maxwell would say, "You either got to go to work or you get to go to work." There is a difference.

- You have to discover your why. In my grandmother's basement, as in the rest of my life, I did many different things, but I always I gravitated towards inspiring people. That is why I was put on this earth. It doesn't matter if I'm working for a corporation or inside the church community or even if I'm working out in the gym. Wherever I am, I aim to inspire, motivate, and to give back. This is my why.

- You must seek what you were put on this earth to do.

Then, pursue it with all your heart. If you decide that good enough is good enough, you'll never be happy. Strive for true happiness. Strive for better than good enough. It won't be easy, but it will be worthwhile.

- Passion gives you energy. If you have no energy, you need to look elsewhere for your passion. Only when you find it will you be able to work harder than you ever thought possible.

How to Find Your Purpose: A Worksheet

People think that discovering your purpose is the hardest part. But I assure you it is not, if you listen to what the world is trying to tell you. Ask yourself:

- What comes easy? What do you love to do? When I was a resident advisor in college, I was able to inspire and motivate people. In my fraternity, I was a leader from the very beginning. In my work, I always had a team under me that I was meant to inspire. I always sought positions of leadership, and most times, I excelled in them. I was always a positive, optimistic person, and that rubbed off on others and drew them to me. Thus, I am naturally a leader, naturally a teacher. Maybe you prefer to work alone? Maybe you're not a people person? Think deeply about what you love to do and what you do naturally. Write it down. Make a list.
- Where have people acknowledged good that you do? When I was seventeen, I was called upon to speak to a large crowd

with no notice. Although I was nervous, the person who asked me knew that I was comfortable in my own skin. She knew I could get up in front of a crowd and deliver an inspiring message. She had no fear, as I did, that maybe I wasn't ready. People always tell me how I was born to teach and lead and speak. Listen to what people tell you. They just may be right.

- What things run in the family? In my family, my grandmother, and my mother played the piano. My aunt played the piano. My sister played the piano. They watched what talent ran through the family and embraced it. But be careful—sometimes this can be misleading. I took piano lessons. I was terrible at it. But my aunt, a few cousins, and my sister were all teachers, and I was an adjunct professor at the college. Teaching was our purpose, and it also ran in the family. Things like this are what I look for when I say to look for things that run in the family.

Every person God creates has gifts.
—*John C. Maxwell*

Write down the answers to the three questions above. Study what you wrote. Show what you wrote to others. Ask for their input and advice. You never know who will speak the words that change your life. Maybe even a stranger or a child. Maybe your purpose will come to you in a vision. Pray on it. Talk on it. Think on it.

Do you now know your purpose? Good! Then it is time to act!

2

NEVER GIVE UP ON YOUR DREAMS

Why Grow? Why Change? Why Persevere?

You cannot win if you do not begin!

Just because we know what we were put on Earth to do, doesn't mean that we have the motivation to do it. If you don't believe in yourself, then you won't bet on yourself.

Knowing your purpose is important, but choosing to act on your purpose can be the hardest part of leading a meaningful and fulfilling life.

Why?

Because making change is hard.

It's easy to stay in that comfortable job, or relationship, or place. It's easy to keep on keeping on with whatever has been okay for a while.

But this chapter—maybe the most important one in this book—is here to tell you that you must move forward. You must not stop. You are worth more than that. You owe it to yourself, to the universe, and to your God to respect your purpose on this earth.

You must go on; you must grow on.

Fortune 500 Companies and the "Perfect" Career

After I graduated from Western Michigan University with a B.S. degree in Interpersonal Communication and Business Administration, my sister Diane got me an interview with General Foods Maxwell House Coffee Division. It was July, 1979. I was 21 years old. In what I was sure would be the first of many triumphs, I got the job.

But there was a problem. Most graduates walked in May. But I had to retake a business class, in which I'd gotten a D.

I wasn't the kind of person to let a little thing like a bad grade stand in my way. After all, I already had a job offer. I went to the dean of the business school and told him my dilemma. He told me it was fine. I could do an independent study. So that's what I did. It felt so good to have solved this problem. Now I was absolutely sure I was on my way. I was a man who knew how to get things done.

Only there was another roadblock. The job was back in Detroit. No problem. I went to live with my mother, her husband, and my oldest sister, Deb. Unfortunately, my mother treated me like the kid before leaving for college, so I got my own place and never looked back. Another problem solved.

Only now, I realized that I didn't like the job at General Foods. I was selling coffee, but it wasn't satisfying. I would sell in suggested orders, not fully knowing that the store would place the order through their wholesaler. I wanted to see immediate results through direct store delivery from the sales pitch to the order being prepared at our warehouse, to its being loaded onto our trucks for delivery, then through the store's backdoor for receiving, and finally onto the selling floor for consumer purchase and consumption.

One day, I was on my hands and knees, doing a merchandise reset in one of my stores in the coffee section of the aisle to my satisfaction. A man appeared, noticed me, and struck up a conversation. He turned out to be a vice president at the Pepsi-Cola company. "Give us a call," he said. "We need people like you."

No matter what you're doing, do it the absolute best you can. Someone will notice.

That man, Bob Bobbitt, became a mentor to me. He took a liking to me. He took a real interest in me not just as an employee or team member, but as a person. He hired me at Pepsi-Cola, and now I was sure that I was on my way to… somewhere. More money, prestige, power—all the things that mattered to me then in my career.

At Pepsi, if I made the sale, I'd take the order, place it, watch it be loaded onto the trucks, then brought onto the sales floor. It was so much more satisfying than my previous job and taught me a lot about leadership. My mentor at Pepsi understood that to truly lead others, one must give them space and real responsibility, and let them celebrate their triumphs. I was the happiest kid in Detroit. I was on my way.

Soon, my mentor left PepsiCo Bottling Group for Coca-Cola Bottlers of Detroit, and he asked me to join him.

At that time, you had the Coca-Cola Company headquartered in Atlanta, Georgia, selling the syrup to the independent bottlers across the country. The bottlers would bottle and then deliver the product to the retailers. Detroit was a major market at the time, but by 1986, the Coca-Cola Company decided to gain more control and formed Coca-Cola Enterprises, Inc. by buying back independent bottlers, including Coca-Cola Bottlers of Detroit.

As a result, Coca-Cola Enterprises, Inc. closed the sales distribution center that I was managing. It was called a RIF, a Reduction in Force.

I was 27 years old, and after five years of steady advancement, I was out of a job.

I had been the Sales Center Manager and was also responsible for managing over 100 people. This was no small thing, especially for someone so young.

Now, I had been given my walking papers.

"You'll find something," they told me as they pushed me out the door. "You're young."

I sued and won, settling out of court.

Two months later, I had a new job at Faygo Beverages, Inc.

in Detroit, Michigan. We sold the famous red pop, orange, root beer. They had heard of me from my previous work with Pepsi and Coke, a lesson in how a good name and solid work ethic can follow you. It was good money, but a lesser title. Again, the president at Faygo at the time took a liking to me. I was twice promoted until I was the manager of marketing. The previous head of marketing had a director title, but not I. This bothered me, but I was rising too fast to care that much. Plus, remember, positive attitude. I always saw the cup as half full.

When my wife received a promotion in Atlanta at the Kraft Foods company, I decided to go along, even though I didn't have a corporate job lined up. I had other plans—which I'll tell you about later in this book. But what's important here is that I ended up back at Coca-Cola Enterprises, Inc. in Atlanta. Now remember, I had sued them. I had signed an agreement, taken the money, and run. But I made contact anyway with the human resources person. When they saw my experience, they were excited. They didn't do any background checking. They passed my résumé on to the higher-ups. Yes, even after I'd sued them. Good thing they didn't check records as carefully back then as they do now!

They called me in—and offered me an entry-level position.

"No thank you," I said.

At that moment, something came over the interviewer. He stepped out to talk to the general manager. Then, they came back. "We've made a new position for you. You'll be the training and development manager."

I liked the sound of that. When I look back at that interview,

I think it had been a test. He could have dismissed me, but I was ready to walk away, and he saw that confidence in me. That confidence would take me far.

I was soon promoted four times.

From there, I moved on to Frito-Lay. And from Frito-Lay, to Hershey. The reasons and details of the moves, we'll talk about later in this book; for now, what's important is that I always found success and advancement. Sure, I hit a roadblock or two, but I always earned respect. Even when things didn't go exactly as planned, they were going well enough for me to have established myself as an important person in the corporate world.

And yet...

I wasn't happy.

This was hard to face, because, as I said, I was a glass-half-full kind of guy.

But eventually, I had to own up to my unhappiness—corporate life wasn't my path. It wasn't my purpose. And until I acknowledged that, I'd never feel fulfilled.

When I trusted God, I found my path.
I've been on different paths before that weren't
God's path.

*

When I trusted my purpose, I found my path.
I've been on different paths before that weren't the path
of my true purpose.

*

When I trusted my instincts, I found my path.
I've been on different paths before that weren't the path
of my true self.

Good vs. Great

The people who get ahead in the world are the ones who look for the circumstances they want, and if they can't find them, they make them. I had always been that person. But when I sat down and was really honest with myself, something wasn't right.

Good is the enemy of great.

I was doing just fine. Things were good. Because of this, I was afraid to shake up my life and the lives of my loved ones in order to pursue my passion and mission in life. But that couldn't go on forever. Like watching for your passion, you need to watch for other signs. Is the world trying to tell you that you're not on the right path? Picture where you are in any area, right now: your career, your life, your faith. Now picture where you want to be. Are they matching up? Are there signs that you might be ready to get off whatever detour you're on, and get back on the main highway?

The answer for me was simple. I knew my purpose: I am called to make deposits in people's lives and to leave a legacy. This was my why. The music can continue after one's own life is over, in the songs one teaches to others. I had to pass my message to people in my company, to my family, to my community, and to my church. I didn't want to leave anything behind on this earth. I wanted to give everything I had earned and everything I had learned to others. This was what made me truly happy and fulfilled.

Leave a legacy in others, and you have truly achieved something lasting.

I had to find a way to make my purpose come to life. I knew the what, and I knew the why. Now, I needed the push, the motivation to move me forward onto the right path.

Know Your What

Remember that career fair, where I was recruiting for talent to come into our company? Those seniors stopping by the booth needed to know what they wanted. They had to be prepared to go after a career in order to get themselves in a position to get offered an opportunity. I was looking for the gleam in their eyes. I wanted to know if they'd done their research. I wanted to see that passion. Those students were the ones who got a chance to have an interview and get an offer.

Now, I had to let myself be that young kid again, wandering around life, not looking to grab the candy out of the baskets, but instead looking for what I really wanted. How long had it been since I'd approached the world with that kind of wonder? With eyes open to opportunities? I knew what passion looked and felt like. I knew I could continue to pour my passion into my role at my job, but I also knew I had more to give. But how? And where?

Know Your Why

I looked to my why. I had a purpose on this earth. I was here to teach, to lead, and to leave a legacy in others. I was able to do that in my career. But what if I could take all that I'd learned in the corporate world and apply it to the spiritual world? This was a revelation to me: **apply the rules of business to the rules of ministry.** Suddenly, it all made sense. Suddenly, I understood fully what I was on this earth to achieve.

Things that hadn't made sense, now made perfect sense.

I would start a ministry.

This wouldn't make my path to achieving my purpose any easier. But it would certainly make it clearer.

Know What's Holding You Back

You're a person with vision. You understand your purpose, and you understand that you must act on your purpose in order to be a fully happy and fulfilled person. You know why you must act. And yet…

…you still do not.

There are many reasons one does not act on their purpose:

- **You care too much about other people's visions of you.**

Other people want you to be something. These are good people, people who love you, such as your parents or your spouse or your children. Often, they want you to be this thing for their own purposes. They want you to make money, because they need money. They want you to be strong in areas in which they're weak. But often, the desires of the people who love you aren't malicious or selfish. People like the status quo. They can't help it. They were taught to believe that a person must be one certain thing and never change. They are used to you the way you are and don't want you to change. And, because we love these people back, their desires are powerful. Sometimes, we allow their wishes to become even more powerful than our own desires.

The excellent book, *The Energy Bus*, by Jon Gordon, explains this phenomenon well. Gordon tells us that we're the driver of our bus. We decide where we want to go. We decide whom we let on board. If we let others drive our bus or plan our route or come along for the ride, even though they weigh us down, then we're not being true to ourselves.

We must, Gordon tells us, speak and articulate our visions so that we decide where the bus goes, not letting our bus become someone else's bus. "My vision for my family life is… My vision for my work life is… My vision for my faith life is…" Say it out loud. Make sure you understand your destination.

Make sure it's your destination.

Desire, vision, and focus move your bus in the right direction.

You can take others along for the ride, but they are just passengers, free to get off whenever they choose. And you can always ask them to disembark. It's your bus, after all.

The important thing is that you're true to your journey; you don't let others steer your path. It's your bus. Treat it that way.

- **The myth of security: the Lord giveth and the Lord taketh away.**

We often think that we cannot act on our true purpose, because we need security. We have families to support. We think that the things we accumulate are important: houses, cars, clothes. We come to believe that we need all these things. Also, we believe that once we have all these things, we have achieved something in life. But security is a false hope. It's the mindset of trying to hold on that makes you miss opportunities, miss growth. You can't take it with you. Give it away.

The Lord giveth and the Lord taketh away. Maybe there's a flood. Maybe there's an earthquake. Or fire. Maybe there's political unrest. Or a stock market crash. Or a robbery. Everything material in this world can be gone in the blink of an eye. There is no such thing on this earth as material security.

Security is mostly a superstition. It does not exist in nature, nor do the children of men as a whole experience it… Avoiding danger is no safer in the long run than outright exposure. The fearful are caught as often as the bold…
Life is either a daring adventure or nothing.
—Helen Keller

Better to tie our importance to our true purpose. Maybe you will become a school teacher, with a low salary, but you will always have the smiles of your students. Maybe you become a street sweeper, with only a broom to your name, but you have the joy of a job well done and the smiles of your neighbors. Whatever your purpose, it is greater than material goods or else it is not a true purpose.

The story of Job is instructive. The devil tells God that Job loves him because God has given Job wealth and abundance. If God took these things away, then Job would curse God. But when God takes everything from Job, he still doesn't curse God. Job realizes that he cannot understand the ways of the Lord, so he accepts his loss, even if he doesn't understand it. This story illustrates many complex components of faith and theology, and I urge you to read and study the story. But for our point here, the story of Job illustrates that one cannot count on keeping anything but their own inner compass. This compass points you toward your purpose in life. If you stay on your path, no one can take it away from you. Your purpose is yours alone and always will be.

- **You don't believe in yourself because of past failures or disappointments.**

To move forward today, you must learn to say goodbye to yesterday's hurts, tragedies, and baggage.

Believe you can, and you're halfway there. Any failure you have experienced was really a lesson to give you the skills you need to move forward. As for any tragedy you experienced—you are still here, aren't you? You survived last time, so why wouldn't you survive again? And weren't you made stronger from your ordeal? Truly, if you survived that, whatever it is—divorce, death of a loved one, a tragedy beyond belief—then surely you can survive the next thing and with greater grace and wisdom.

Don't let your past weigh you down. Let it raise you up.

The Mindset of Continual Change

"Either you got to go to work or you get to go to work."
—*John C. Maxwell*

If you got to go to work, then it's time for a change. You need to follow your passion and your purpose.

When your purpose is greater than your challenges, you succeed.

If you continue to show up every day, you'll show improvement.

You have to love it. When you love it you get to go to work.

If you don't love it, you won't put in the time to overcome all of the challenges… even when the world says you should.

You can't take it with you.

You can't take material things, but you also can't take your wisdom. Leave it all behind with others, and you've truly left a legacy.

The Rubberband Law of Life

John C. Maxwell talks about the Rubber Band Law in his excellent book, *The 15 Invaluable Laws of Growth*. The law is simple: "Growth stops when you lose the tension between where you are and where you could be." In other words, you must keep stretching in order to achieve. As Maxwell points out, rubber bands, like people, are useful only when they're stretched.

Next Steps

Now that you know your purpose, now that you have the inspiration to pursue your purpose, we're faced with another hard question: how does one pursue one's purpose?

Luckily, many great minds have pondered this question. The answer has four parts. None are easy, but all are necessary. The sooner you get started, the better. No matter where you are on your life's journey, the important thing is to start, and then to let nothing stop you. You got this. Don't stop now.

3

YOU ARE A DIAMOND IN THE ROUGH. THERE IS NONE OTHER LIKE YOU.

How to Grow Into Your Purpose

Step 1: Education

Great leaders must be great learners.
In order to lead, you need knowledge.

At six years old, a proud first-grader at the red-bricked Winterhalter Elementary School, I hit my first educational roadblock. My mother was told I had a reading deficiency. My grandmother would have none of that. We were an educated family, a family of professionals and soon-to-be scholars. She took it upon herself to teach me to read. Naturally, she opened her favorite book in the world, The Bible. "Son," she said, "read."

I read.

I got back on track with the regular class within the year.

I never really believed that reading had been my problem, or at least, not my main problem. I had more energy than most kids. Today, I'd be called hyperactive and maybe given medicine. Instead, my mother gave me chores to do after school. At six years old, I cleaned and did yard work. I handled the laundry and the ironing. It gave me structure and a way to use my energy.

Still not satisfied, my mother insisted that I change my appearance. From then on, I wore a shirt and tie to school. At the time, during elementary school, we didn't have a lot. I remembered I had two pairs of pants, one blue and the other black. I washed and ironed them every day.

All of this made me calmer, more studious. It gave me focus. I was learning that I could fix my own problems with discipline and resolve.

Adversity makes us stronger.

In the third grade (we called it 3B and 3A back then), I got Scarlet Fever in the 3A. I was quarantined and had to stay home. I missed so much school that I "failed" 3A. I watched all my friends move on to 4B, while I had to stay behind.

I vowed to fix my predicament over the summer. While the other kids played ball and enjoyed other summer activities, I enrolled in summer school, riding my bike each way every day. I made my own lunch. I was eight years old, but I understood that I was responsible for my future and myself. It worked. I caught up with my friends.

Now, I cared about grades. School was important to me. Grades mattered. I never wanted to fall behind again.

My aunt Mae saw that I was determined to get ahead, and she hired a tutor for me. Her colleagues helped me when I didn't understand some math concept or complicated science theory. I think they saw in me a future educator, someone who loved learning for learning's sake. They knew I was a teacher at heart. This was also when my basement "teaching" sessions that I described earlier began. My life was starting to fall into a pattern.

Along with secular school, I was also being educated in the Methodist church. I'd go with my grandmother every Sunday, I participated in church and attended Sunday school serving as a youth usher and junior trustee. But something was missing. I never truly had a personal relationship with God. I got water baptized, but I didn't know the significance of it. I was too young to understand.

When I was seventeen, I was in church for a youth revival. The speaker, another young person, got cold feet and pulled out. The woman organizing the event said, "Charles, you're going to be the speaker tonight."

I had no warning. No time for preparation—or for fear. I turned to the Book of Genesis, the story of Abraham and Isaac: Trust in God.

That was an eye-opener.

I had butterflies, but I trusted in God. I went up in front of that crowd, and I spoke.

From that point onward, I became more involved.

Now, I was training for a future in the church community. Four years later, I would enter ministry training at the age of 21 and would one day become a church elder and a Youth Pastor.

Yet, before that could occur, after only four years of training, I walked away, because I didn't think I measured up to such a high calling. I was done. I thought that to be a minister, I had to be perfect. I wasn't perfect. I had lost my virginity. I believed that I wasn't living up to the calling of a truly Godly man. I continued learning in the corporate world. I continued my secular education, earning my Master's in Management and Supervision from Central Michigan University.

I wouldn't come back to complete ministry training for another four years because I believed I had to be perfect or close to being perfect. I didn't realize that we are all diamonds in the rough. Just as an employer doesn't expect you to know all the ropes when you first take a job, God doesn't expect perfection and all-knowingness when you enter His realm. I hadn't noticed the steps that others took before me to educate themselves, to learn, and then to make themselves better along the way; I was just a diamond in the rough that needed polishing. It's not easy, as a diamond is the hardest substance on Earth.

Just like a diamond, a person is hard and doesn't yield easily to outside force.
A person is set in stone, stubborn to change his or her form.
It takes time, patience, and a trained hand to mold a diamond into its most beautiful, valuable form.

For a diamond, it takes a knife.
For a person, it takes education.

In 1987, I was 30 years old. I made an appointment with my pastor. I explained to him that I was compelled to come back and resume ministerial training and enroll in seminary. I felt my purpose, and I couldn't stay away. I picked up where I left off, though I worried that I had lost too much time. But we're all on our own paths. No two people walk the same path, at the same pace, toward the same destination. It didn't matter that I'd taken the break, only that I had returned.

It's never too late to be what you might have been.
—_George Eliot_

I became a Licensed Minister. But I didn't stop there. A year after that, I was ordained as Deacon and as an Elder.

But something was still missing in my life, and I honestly had no idea what it was. Everyone told me I was on my way to doing great things, that I had a great future in the church and in my career.

April 14, 1989, I was at a revival for adults. I was a minister, in a robe, sitting in the pulpit. Just an ordinary day. When it came time for the altar call, I got up and kneeled at the altar rail with several others. I didn't know why, I just felt compelled. I came to face the pulpit, eyes closed. The revivalist preacher prayed over us. When he finished, he said, "If there is anyone here who feels they need additional prayer, stay."

I stayed, my eyes still closed.

I could hear people leaving all around me.

Why am I here? Kneeling in this minister's robe? I had no idea.

"Brother, what is it?" the preacher asked.

I looked up. There were tears streaming down my face. At that exact moment, I had a conversion life-changing experience. It was the day I received Christ in my life. That night, I humbled myself before all in attendance. I went from doing good works in the church to a heartfelt change in my total being.

From that moment on, I became more sensitive to my calling and to God leading me along my personal journey.

My grandmother had led me to give the pastor my hand, but not to give my heart to God, through no fault of my grandmother's. I realized then that it was me who was standing between the old me and the new me. I had to make the decision to open my heart, not to judge myself, but to love myself.

This attitude holds true in the business world, too. We feel that we're not perfect, and so we don't deserve that raise or that promotion. You must walk away from that attitude.

"Better a diamond with a flaw than a pebble without."
—Confucius

A year later, I was ordained as an Elder. But I had no intention of stopping there. A year after that, I graduated from Ashland Theological Seminary with a Master's in Religious Studies. But I had no intention of stopping there; some years later, I returned to

Ashland Seminary for my doctorate degree. I was working full-time in Detroit, and all the while working towards my doctorate degree in Ashland, Ohio. My classes were longer than a three-hour drive from Detroit, and even further from Atlanta, where my family had recently relocated.

Didn't matter. I wasn't stopping now. If I was going to educate others, I must educate myself first.

I received my doctorate degree in Transformational Leadership from Ashland Theological Seminary in 2008. My thesis, *Disciple to Discipler*, a concept I'll explain more about in the second half of this book, became the bedrock of my beliefs and my life.

I was finally, at 50 years old, Dr. Charles Redd. Jr.

But in truth, the majority of the most important elements of my educational journey hadn't happened in school at all.

Two Paths to One Destination

While I pursued my religious education, I also continued my education in my corporate career. I was starting to realize that both the church culture and the corporate culture could transform people's lives. I was also realizing that what you study is what you become. My mother, at that time, was watching a lot of news on the television. She was studying the news. And when she talked, she became a newsreel. It was what made her happy.

I was happy studying positivity, because that's what I wanted to be: a positive leader.

And, I began not just to study leadership, but to apply it, both in the corporate world and in the church.

If you study leadership,
you become a better leader and influencer.

But what is a leader, really, and how do you find a leader in your life? It's an important concept, because to truly change your life, to truly be an educated person, you need companionship. You can't do it alone, and you can't do it with only formal schooling.

Everyone Needs a Paul, Barnabus, and Timothy

- A Paul is someone mature in your life, who pours wisdom into you.
- A Barnabus is a co-laborer. He's on the journey as an encourager, as iron sharpens iron, each making one another better and determined to succeed.
- A Timothy is an understudy, someone newer, with lesser experience than you, whom you can raise up, pour into.

You reach up. You reach across. You reach down.
In this way, you are always educating yourself,
encouraging others, and educating others.

My Paul, Barnabus, and Timothy (My Mentors, My Co-laborers, and My Mentees)

The people you need, appear. It's hard to say why or how, but they show up when you need them.

Reverend Mary Watson Stewart was my spiritual mother. She knew my grandmother, and that was how I met her. After my grandmother passed in 1986, she adopted me as her spiritual son. She was always supportive and loving. I could talk to her about anything. She gave me so much wisdom during my hardest times. She'd listen, providing advice and unconditional love, but she'd also provide tough love. She'd say, *there's your side, the other side, and the truth.*

She was also a teacher in the literal sense: she taught school. She married a medical doctor and went into ministry as an evangelist. She went from church to church, spreading the gospel, her knowledge, and her love. She was a genuine elder, respected by her peers.

At the end of her life, fading in her hospital bed, she told her caregiver, Martha, "I want Elder Redd to do my eulogy." She knew everyone, but she chose me. I made a special trip to pray over her, to read scripture over her. But the Bishop Robert Thomas, Jr., my former pastor, asked me to move over out of respect for the bishop and let him do the honors. Not a month later, the bishop passed away. Before he died, he thanked me for allowing him to do Mother Stewart's eulogy.

Mother Stewart had reminded me of grandmother. She took over the role of my grandmother after my grandmother was gone. She was human. She was my teacher. I learned more from her than from any formal teacher I've ever had.

Rev. Amelia Dortch was my co-laborer, my peer. She stepped into the role of my older sister, Deb, after Deb passed away in

1990. Amelia was there to help fill the void. We attended seminary together. We were ordained elders together. Mother Stewart brought us to her side together. Mother Stewart was, in the spirit of Paul, a spiritual mom to both of us. We'd have long, endless conversations over tea and cake, then take the conversations back to our own ministry, family, and workplaces. We'd even have Thanksgiving dinner at her home. These were my time-out moments.

We gave each other encouragement and prayer.

Iron sharpens iron. There's something in you I need, and something in me you need, and if we connect and share, we sharpen each other.

When Mother Stewart grew older and wasn't able to get around as she used to, Sister Amelia and I would do nice things for her. We'd read scriptures to her. Minister to one another. She viewed us as daughter and son to her. She was well-to-do, and certainly didn't need our help, as she had a live-in caretaker, but we would provide some assistance for her anyway.

Another important mentor to me was **Presiding Elder Martin Luther Simmons**. He was another leader from the church whom my grandmother admired. I remember him preaching a sermon when I was a young teenager: "I will trust in the Lord." He's the one who signed off on my license to preach. He heard me pray during service one time and paid me a compliment and said, "You pray with sincerity."

When he died, I kept his obituary.

- You grow when you hang around people who are constant learners and knowers.
- You grow when you make learning your lifetime endeavor.
- We all have room to grow. A leader who loves the status quo soon becomes a follower.
- We become educated in school, in career, and in life. All offer opportunities to learn.

*

What education will you pursue? Reading this book is a good start. Now, what will you do next to further educate yourself? Another book? A class? A degree? Will you educate yourself in business? In your spiritual life? In your personal life? These are all worthy and important arenas for gaining knowledge. Pursue whatever you choose with purpose and seriousness. You deserve to educate yourself. Take the time and make the investment in yourself.

Who are your mentors? If you don't have any, you need to find some. Who is on a similar journey to yours? Reach out to them so they can walk beside you. You do not need to take this journey alone. Who is behind you? Turn around and reach out to them. They are looking to you for answers. Open your eyes and heart, and you will find people around you who want to help you and educate you and people who need your help and your knowledge.

Take action.

Don't turn the page until you decide what exactly you're going to do.

Make a list. Share it with others. Dedicate yourself to the task.

Now that you understand the importance of education, you understand the importance of never stopping learning, you've taken the first step toward your purpose.

But this is not enough to achieve your purpose. Now you're ready for Step Two.

You need a plan.

No problem. Let's get started!

4

LIFE IS ABOUT SETTING AND ACHIEVING GOALS

How to Achieve Your Purpose

Step 2: Making a Plan and Sticking to It

You were born to win, but to be a winner, you must plan to win, prepare to win, and expect to win.

—Zig Ziglar

I once mentored a young man in the music field. He was struggling as a server at a restaurant. He was making CDs, hoping to get his chance. It was hard for him to believe in himself, when the odds were stacked against him.

I told him, "You have this gift. Keep moving. You're going to get there."

This man was focused on one goal, but it was a hard goal, a long goal, the kind of goal that wouldn't happen overnight. So the challenge here was to build his courage and his conviction, while also setting smaller goals. Make that CD. Book that gig. If the goal is fame and fortune, he wasn't going to sustain himself. He needed small victories along the way.

> *Life is about setting goals. Personal goals, professional goals, and spiritual goals.*
> *Get the big picture first, then break it down.*
> *You can't eat an elephant in one bite, but you can, bite-by-bite, in small pieces.*

I was in a different situation, further along my path in life. I had more education, more experience, and more connections. So I was able to have six buckets on my desk: six big goals. Could I really make a plan for each one, a step-by-step plan, and achieve them all? I had my corporate career, to which I had to give 110 percent . I had my purpose in life—to form a ministry. I had my speaking goals. And my personal goals. And my fitness goals. And my relationship goals. (I'll talk more about each of these later in the book. For now, let's just say—I had a lot to get done).

I could do it because I broke the big goals down into small goals, and also because I had the Redd Team: friends and family and other helpers I'd brought together to help me achieve my goals. Each person had a task. I encouraged, brought it all together like an orchestra leader. I was reaching in the three directions, up and out and down, in order to get more knowledge, trade knowledge, and give knowledge. In this way, my team and I moved forward, step-by-step, toward our goals.

You have to decide for yourself how many balls you can keep in the air at once. Or better, you need to have a mentor or a friend sit down with you and help you decide what you can manage. Do you have a small child or spouse or other family member who needs your constant attention? That will make a difference in how many goals you can handle at once. Do you have funds available to hire people who can help you with your goals? That will also make a big difference. If you don't have funds to pay people, do you have friends you can tap to be your helpers and your support? Do you have things to offer them, so that helping you isn't about you, but is also about moving them forward on their paths?

Decide exactly what goal (or goals) you want to achieve, then focus on the goal(s) and only the goal(s).
Be willing to put in the work, and then re-assess if there's too much on your plate—or too little!

How to Make a Plan

Planning your life is about finding yourself, knowing who you are, and then customizing a design for your growth. You can't just sit on the couch, thinking about your goals and your purpose. If you're taking a literal journey, say, traveling from Atlanta to Los Angeles by car, then you know it's two thousand miles. You wouldn't just get in your car and go. You'd do the math: how many miles can you go in a day? You'd break it down: where would be fun to stop? To eat? To rest? Who do you want to see along the way? Friends? Family? Are there sites worth stopping at? Now, you've broken down the journey into parts, into small pleasures and achievable segments. Now you know what to expect on the journey. You know how much gas you'll need and how much money you have, so you won't get stuck on the side of the highway in Montana. You know how your car's been acting—maybe you get it tuned up first—so you know if those front tires are going to make the journey to the end. You know who to call if you get a flat, or that you have the tools in the trunk to fix it yourself, so if you're in the desert, you won't have to wait too long in the sun. Is that spare inflated? Do you have water and a first aid kit in case you slip and cut your hand? You're ready for anything, now! You know how this trip is going to go. And if you decide to get off on an exit at the spur of the moment—you got that, too. You know your end goal, so you'll have the motivation and know-how to get back on the highway.

Planning to achieve your purpose in life is just like planning a literal trip. There's a lot to think about, but don't let it stop you. Let it excite you. You don't want to get stuck in the same old place for your whole life. There's a whole world out there. You want to move on. You want to go places. I'm going to show you how.

If you go to work on your goals, your goals will go to work on you. If you go to work on your plan, your plan will go to work on you. Whatever good things we build end up building us.

—Jim Rohn

Step 1: Set the Goal

You're wondering: *wait a minute Dr. Charles, didn't we already set our purpose in chapter one? We found our vision and acknowledged that we had a pull in life, a purpose that could not be denied.*

Yes. We did this. But a purpose is not a goal. A goal needs to be concrete. Achievable. Defined.

My **purpose** in life is to inspire, motivate, and give to others; to teach, to make deposits in people in order to leave a legacy.

My **goal** is threefold:

1. to achieve my purpose in my professional career by **practicing transformational leadership** (more on that later) and raising up others to achieve their goals and become corporate leaders.
2. to achieve my purpose by **speaking** to others within corporate America, educational school systems, and the church community.
3. **to create a ministry** based on transformational leadership, where the spiritual community supports one another.

My purpose can be broken down into concrete, actionable goals:

*   When I help people whom I supervise at work to get promoted, I have achieved a concrete, tangible goal.
*   When I book an event and get up on that stage to speak, I have achieved a concrete, tangible goal.

- When I form my ministry, and create a community of faith, I have achieved a concrete, tangible goal.

In order to transform your purpose into your goal, think on ways to translate it into action, a thing that exists in the world, outside your mind. Write it down. Journal about it. What does success look like? Draw an actual picture of what success looks like—even if you can't draw! The point isn't to make art, but to make progress! If you can't bring yourself to draw, look on the Internet. Cut out pictures and make a collage. This is your inspiration board. Look at that picture. Put it on the wall. It's a motivator. It's something real and tangible to set your sights on.

My inspiration board might be of my team, climbing the ladder of success. It might be of speakers I admire with huge crowds spread out before them. Or corporations where I want to speak: exact churches or auditoriums or even stadiums—why not? Gotta dream big to win big! Maybe I have another inspiration board of ministries and ministers I admire. If you want to lose weight, maybe your pictures are of people who have already achieved that goal. If your purpose is to write a book, maybe your pictures are of books you love, or maybe even of your book, with your title and your name already on the cover.

Once you can see it clearly, you know exactly what it is you want to bring into this world. You can make it real.

Step 2: Share the Dream

This is often the hardest part of planning. Why is it so hard to tell other people what you intend to achieve? Is it because you think you may not achieve it, and then you'd be embarrassed? But this is the best reason of all to share your vision with others. When I share, I put pressure on myself—soft pressure. If I hide it, I may give up. A little chagrin isn't always the worst thing.

The second reason to tell others is that you cannot achieve your goals alone. The people you tell will serve as resources. They'll be your contacts, your supporters, your network.

a) Tell people who won't judge, so it's safe. These people will help you to gain confidence. This may be your mentor, co-workers, or friends, or even just the person you see every week at the gym. Formulating the words to express what you plan to do will help you with your goal, even if the other person doesn't have much to say. Just hearing yourself say, "I'm going to quit my job and move to Albuquerque and start that llama farm" makes it more real—or allows you to hear if you sound ridiculous, even to yourself. Do you need to revise your goal? Now is a good time. Maybe you'll move to Albuquerque and open the doggie day care to get some experience with animals first. Now it sounds better, even to you. Listening and speaking the actual words brings them into the world. It makes the goal manifest.

When people you tell give you support, accept it. Take their enthusiasm and enjoy it. People who love you want you to succeed. They want you to be happy. And remember, you're also helping them. By demonstrating the process of making goals and sharing goals, maybe they'll do the same for themselves. Maybe next time you see them, they'll confide their goals in you. Support them.

Encourage them. Raise them up. None of us can make this journey alone.

b) Once you have confidence, branch out. Talk to experts in the field. Ask for feedback. You now want to tell your goal to people who have experience, so they can help you see your missteps. They can help you regroup. They can tell you what you still need to learn and what steps they took to get them where they are.

Talking to experts often requires a leap of faith: why on earth would these people be willing to talk to me? But here's the thing about successful people: they didn't get successful by magic. They had people help them on their way up the ladder. They remember being in the position you're in now, so they empathize with and understand your dilemma. And who knows, think positive: if they take a liking to you and see something in you, they may even offer to mentor you.

Also, remember that people like to be seen as experts. You're appealing to their ego, and that's hard to resist. Remember when I told you earlier about my friend who had too many people asking him for favors? One reason he would accept was because it stoked his ego to be told that he was needed, that he was important, and that they needed his help. We all like to be needed. Nothing wrong with that. That's just human nature.

Ask people for advice.
The worst thing that can happen is that they say no.
The world won't catch on fire. The sky won't fall.

***You'll walk one way, and they'll walk another,
and you will find someone else who will say yes.***

c) Tell your accountability partners.

Who are your accountability partners? They're people whom you ask for help. Friends or coworkers or others from the community. Or, maybe they're professionals whom you pay. These people form a pact with you to hold you to your goals.

One way we're often familiar with accountability partners is at the gym. Exercising alone is hard. You have to show up. And then, once you're there, you have to work hard and not slack off. But this is hard to do by yourself. Some days, you're tired. Some days, you're sleepy. Some days, you feel you've worked too hard the day before, and you're too sore. So you can skip today, who cares? No one will even notice!

But if you have a personal trainer, or an accountability partner, then you have to show up. And once you get there, you have to perform. This person is in your face, encouraging you, telling you what to do and also rooting you on, telling you that you can do it.

Even more important than this, when you're done, this person celebrates with you. This doubles the pleasure so that you're more willing to come back and work hard the next time. Maybe even twice as hard, because what you've just achieved feels so good.

Just like in the gym, for our health, we can have accountability partners in life, for our goals. Whether it's a life coach or a friend or a minister or a boss, you'll check in with this person regularly for the express purpose of discussing your progress. Even better if the person can discuss their goals back with you. When I decided to share my purpose with my daughter, she became one of my most valuable accountability partners. She even stepped in to help, aligning her goals with mine so that she took over one of my projects, and I was able to help her move forward on hers.

Step 3: Break It Down Into Small Steps You Can Measure

A friend of mine was heavy. Okay, he was obese. He tried medicine of all kinds. Nothing worked. But finally, he decided it was time to change. He started with putting on his gym shoes and showing up at the gym for fifteen minutes. Just to go. Maybe he wouldn't exercise at all. Or maybe he'd just do a slow walk on the treadmill to get the feel of it, nothing more.

Then he expanded to twenty minutes. He was getting used to showing up now. It wasn't so bad. He was getting the hang of the treadmill. He was able to walk a little faster now, use the controls more easily.

Then, 30 minutes. Now he knew the route to the gym, where the traffic light was too long, so he could avoid it, and where the traffic backed up, so he could alter his route. He had a favorite treadmill, so he felt at home. He had picked out the workout music that he liked best, so he had that to look forward to, as well. He had a few regulars who said hello and goodbye to him.

He started seeing results.

In addition, he started liking what he was doing. It was becoming part of his routine. It gave him pleasure to be a person who showed up, a part of the gym community.

Now, he's half the person he was. No more high cholesterol pills. No more missing work for being too sick to get there.

He inspired me. I started looking at my workout the way he looked at his. Sure, I wasn't obese. In fact, I loved the gym. I was in great shape. But still, why not break down my workout into steps like my friend did? With that in mind, I could also add a little more each day. What was I capable of achieving if I thought like that?

- **Set small steps with measurable results.** From just arriving, to more minutes spent in the gym, to quality time, to achievement, my friend could constantly achieve and know that he'd achieved. Measurement makes a difference. You need to have a way to evaluate progress, to judge results, and to diagnose problems.

- **Make lists of plans and of results.** With everything he had to do on one sheet of paper, he could be sure he had no excuses not to achieve his goal. He had clean gym clothes ready to go (check!), had a full water-bottle (check!), had a set goal to achieve, for example, 30 minutes on the treadmill (check!). He also had lists of his goals, so that he could be sure he was accountable to them, too. For example, he would lose five pounds (check!), ten pounds (check!), 50 pounds (check!).

Never underestimate the value of lists.

Step 4: Take the First Step, Then Keep on Moving Forward

We can have dreams, we can have plans, we can have partners, and we can have lists, but unless we act, we'll never achieve our purpose. What do you have to lose by taking the first step?

Take some quiet time to build your resolve.

Take time to think.

Remind yourself: Life is about setting goals, big goals and small goals. You've set yourself up with the magic of structure. You've built the plan to make this work. You've gathered your allies. Now, it's time to act. You've never done this before. You don't know if it will work. Despite your education, your passion, your plan, your allies, and your motivation, you're still wondering: wouldn't it be easier to just forget all this? Turn on the TV and relax back on the couch?

I urge you not to do that.

That is an action, too.

An action in the wrong direction.

The one action that will fill you with regret.

So if you're going to take action anyway, why not go in the right direction?

What you need now is to stop listening to your mind, and listen to your heart.

You can do this.

You're so close.

Don't you dare stop now.

5

LIFE'S TWISTS AND TURNS: THE LEAP OF FAITH

How to Achieve Your Purpose

Step 3: The Leap of Faith

When you get to the end of all the light you know and it's time to step into the darkness of the unknown, faith is knowing that one of two things shall happen: either you will be given something solid to stand on, or you will be taught how to fly.

—*Edward Teller*

In 2004, my wife and I decided to split up after 23 years of marriage. Things had been going badly in our relationship for a while, but we had held it together for my daughter's sake until she left for college. I'll talk more about the divorce later, and about what that did to my confidence and my resolve and how it affected my purpose in life. But this chapter is about something different: taking a leap of faith.

I was at a low point in my life.

What next? My daughter was setting out on the journey of her own life, away from home at school at the University of North Carolina at Chapel Hill, and I wished her well. But now, with my wife and I splitting, I was in Detroit alone. I was lonely. I had doubts. I was sad and disappointed that things had not turned out as I thought they would.

I decided to return to Atlanta where I had some previous success, great friends, and a fresh start.

It was a leap of faith.

I had no job waiting for me there, but I was going to leap. I started to search for another career opportunity.

I had nowhere to live, but I was going to leap. I purchased a home in Atlanta, even though I still owned my home in Detroit. I put my Detroit house on the market (another leap of faith), and to my relief, it quickly sold.

One day, when I was at my house in Detroit getting things packed to move, an interesting thing happened. Everything was just about packed up, ready to go. I was in the process of giving most things away, because I wanted to start over fresh in Atlanta. Suddenly, I heard a knock on the door. It was nighttime, so it was strange for someone to knock at this hour.

I cautiously went to the door and peered out.

A woman stood on the porch. She looked vaguely familiar, but I couldn't place her.

She said, "I saw the porch light on and decided to knock. My husband and I bought your home, and I was wondering if I could come in and take some measurements for furniture."

"Sure, come on in."

We got to talking while she measured. When I told her I was donating almost everything, she offered to buy some of the furniture that I was planning to take with me. I asked her about herself, and she told me that she worked for the Frito-Lay company and was relocating to Detroit for a job promotion.

On a whim, I blurted out, "Could you help me get a job in Atlanta with Frito-Lay?"

What audacity! Where had that come from?

I think we were both a little shocked at my forthrightness.

I have no idea why I asked her for help. Maybe because I'd been practicing asking people for help in my quest to achieve my purpose. I knew by then that things didn't happen when you worked alone. I was used to reaching out.

Or maybe, I was just so low after the divorce that I'd have done anything to get myself back on track.

In any case, whatever the reason for my speaking up, she paused for just a moment, looked at me quizzically, then smiled and said, "Sure."

She wrote a letter of recommendation to a regional vice president she knew at Frito-Lay in Atlanta, Georgia, and he hired me.

That is what following your purpose, following God, is all about. Your purpose is a promise, but there's always twists and turns.

Things don't happen in a straight line. But in the end, if you risk, He provides. If you take the leap, then God, or life, or the universe, or whatever it is you believe in, will catch you.

How do I know? Well, you're still here, aren't you? You've never fallen so badly that you couldn't get back up. Experience teaches us that we can survive.

There are so many things we can't understand in this world. People say to me, *Dr. Charles, you're not 62. I would never have guessed it.* It always amazed me, too. Why do I look younger than my age? Now that I know my purpose, I believe God is keeping me young to be presented to others. I'll be relevant and able, despite my age, to deliver His message. Things that you don't understand will eventually be revealed to you. Until they are, you have to trust and keep moving forward.

You can't always know what to do, but you sense what to do—a sixth sense. You're walking down the street, and something tells you to cross the street. You do, and suddenly, a brick falls off a building right into the path of where you would have been walking. You acted on faith and were rewarded.

Once, I was driving down the highway. A tractor trailer was ahead of me in the next lane. Something told me, *Move over.* Now. I switched to the far-left lane. The truck veered into my lane, where I had been driving just a split second before. It would have run me down.

These sorts of situations happen all the time: a taxi driver won't pick up fare, a mother's intuition tells her to pick up her kids early from school, or a wife just knows.

We shouldn't ignore these moments or treat them as luck. Like having a purpose, we feel the pull of necessity, of the universe, of God, of experience, of whatever we want to call it, and so we act, even if we don't know why. This is a fact of life.

> *A possibility is a hint from God. One must follow it.*
> —*Soren Kierkegaard*

Give Up Control

Taking a leap of faith is an admission that we don't control everything in life. We have a purpose, we get educated, we make a plan, but then things can happen that we couldn't ever have prepared for. It is at times like these that faith steps in.

Twelve years ago, I was on a plane. There was a storm brewing. I noticed that the pilot was making a faster-than-normal, steep descent to land. The wind was blowing. I was wondering why he was trying to land this plane in this condition. The pilot had a choice: whether to try to fly above it or to land. As the wind picked up viciously around us, I thought, why is he trying to land? It felt like the wrong decision.

I could hear the children around me screaming. I could feel their fear. I prayed for the pilots and the crew and the passengers. I had no control. I wasn't the pilot. I closed my eyes and gave myself over to faith. In the midst of it all, I heard clearly between my ears that we would be fine and land safely.

This is often how life is. In times of emergency, of great stress, of uncertainty, you hand it over. You trust in God or the universe or common humanity or maybe just your gut. You trust that someone or something will step in and save you when you need it most. You do this because you have to. You have no choice. But life is full of these moments, and they almost always work out.

The pilot landed that plane. The instant we pulled into the gate, the storm exploded around us. It was a moment I'll never forget. It was a moment that happened over and over in my life in various ways.

Pray, trust, then close your eyes and leap.

A ship in harbor is safe, but that is not what ships are built for.
—*John A. Shedd*

Abraham and Isaac and the Leap of Faith

When God told Abraham to take his son Isaac to the top of the mountain and sacrifice him, Abraham didn't want to. He didn't understand why he had to do such a difficult thing. But he took the leap of faith. He did as he was commanded. At the last moment, right before the sacrifice, God stepped in and told him to sacrifice a ram, instead. Abraham had proven himself faithful, ready to leap, even if he didn't understand why.

There are three steps in the story of Abraham that can be instructive in our lives:

1) The Promise

In the beginning of the story of Abraham, God made Abraham a promise: pick up from your comfortable life and go to a distant land where he would become the founder of a nation and a leader of people. God told Abraham, *I'll be there with you. I'm going to defend you. I'm going to bless you. I'm going to reveal myself. I will give you a son.* It was a huge promise. Abraham had been living in comfort with community, family, and friends. Abraham had a choice. He could stay where he was with the security he had. Or, he could take the step to the next place, even though the outcome was uncertain.

When I think about my own experience and background, God came to me, and he made promises. The promise was my purpose. I was very excited to open myself to this opportunity. Know that your purpose in life is God's promise. You must do this thing, and fulfill your purpose; that's why you were put on this earth.

I was in Detroit, comfortable, living, working. But God challenged me. He called me out. He showed me the promise. He showed me the vision. He showed me my purpose. But this was only the first step.

2) The Sacrifice

God does not say, go forward and take this risk, and I'll make everything easy for you. God's promise does not include the promise of ease, good times, and freely giving. Being separated from your home, your comfort zone, is hard. You want to feel secure. But you won't always have that feeling that everything is wonderful. God expects a person to yield to His lead and to trust Him.

Many believers today see that when they make up their minds to surrender and follow God, they almost always encounter a test. Remember this: God tests; the devil tempts. The test will require commitment. It will require sacrifice. But these tests and the sacrifice give us strength. Without them, we would not be ready to accept the promise.

- Temptation is the devil, or the detour from your purpose. It's the easy way out.
- Tests are about your faith in God, the universe, or even your faith in yourself.
- No easy crossing is promised to anyone, ever. If fulfilling one's purpose was easy, then everyone would do it. Look around you. So many people have lost their way.

3) The Leap of Faith

Moses and the Red Sea crossing is another story of faith, of having nowhere to turn. Moses led his people out of Egypt to the banks of the Red Sea. The Pharaoh and his army were close behind. Moses's people asked him, *Why did you bring us here into the desert to be slaughtered?* Moses didn't know, but he had faith. God parted the waters, and the people walked through to safety while the waters closed in on the Pharaoh's army.

Lean not into your own understanding, but acknowledge God and He shall direct your path.

—*Prov. E, Verses 5–6*

Leap Alone; Land With Others

A non-believer would say, *if I don't have faith in God, then how can I take a leap of faith? I don't have faith.*

Another way to have faith is to believe in people. It's amazing, that when you need people most, they find you. They come alongside you. Maybe you're on the highway, and someone calls to you, "Hey, your tire is flat."

So you pull over. Maybe the next person pulls up in front of you. "You need help changing that tire? I can't help you, but I can lend you the tools."

Now, a third person comes. "Good thing you have the tools. I can use them to change that tire for you." People appear:

- **To plant a seed:** telling you what you need to hear at that moment, pointing you in the direction of what you need to do; revealing your path, your next steps.
- **To water the seed:** to provide you with the tools to take the next step that you couldn't have taken alone.
- **To harvest the seed:** to help you directly in your purpose.

People appear when you most need them, then most of them move on. Maybe you'll never see them again. But maybe they'll stick around and become your companion for life. Maybe next time, you'll be one of those people to someone else: the speaker of truths, the supplier of skills, or the helper and holder. Life will teach you at some point—sickness, job loss, flat tire—that you need someone. And also that you are needed. Learn it sooner rather than later. Family friends, professionals, strangers: all these people can be forces in your life. So when you leap, you never land alone.

And if people don't step in? If we feel all the people in our lives are gone? If we feel we are truly alone? If we say, *Everyone abandoned me. I'm helpless.* Then God comes in. Then, there is divine intervention. Keep living, and you'll have an experience that lets you learn this simple truth.

Again, if you don't believe it, I have proof: you are still here, aren't you? You are still striving? So you've never been let to fall off a cliff too steep to handle.

Great things happen when we stop seeing ourselves as God's gift to others and begin seeing others as God's gift to us.

—*James S. Vuocolo*

The Story of John and Peter and the Beggar

John and Peter were outside the church when a beggar approached and asked for silver and gold. They replied that they had no gold or silver, but they asked the beggar to look up at them. Then, they said to him, "Rise up and walk."

The beggar did not expect this result. He was looking for a handout, not a hand up.

What he got from John and Peter was the greatest gift of all, but it was not the gift he expected.

We, like the beggar, must be open to possibilities. People, or God, or the universe, won't always be there to give us what we want and what we expect, but they may just give us something greater: that thing we truly need.

Another Leap of Faith is Giving to Others

At another low point in my life and my career, I was, for reasons we'll discuss later, done with my job at Frito-Lay making the decision to return to Atlanta. I went online and saw that The Hershey Company was hiring. I applied online: a needle in a haystack.

While I waited to hear back and to see what life had in store for me next, I had time on my hands. I was watching a TBN network preacher. He preached a message on faith. At the end of the message, I was moved to make a donation. Part of me was saying, no I cannot afford to at this time. But another part was telling me just to do it. I called and made a $1,000 donation on my credit card. I knew if I wrote a check, I'd never send it.

It was less than a week later when I received communication from The Hershey Company for an interview. Shortly after, I was hired.

It had been an act of faith to apply to The Hershey Company, and then to give that money away. In a natural sense, it didn't make any sense. But when I do unconventional things, take that leap, things happen. I was led by the Spirit. We have to make room in our lives for stepping outside of what's obvious and rational. There are so many things that we don't understand.

Another way to look at that story is to see the leap of faith as a way to draw positive energy toward yourself. When you're feeling down, you let bad thoughts in. But you need to be positive to let the light in. If you take a positive action, any positive action, it moves the energy around us.

Just the very act of letting go of money, or some other treasure does something within us. It destroys the demon greed.
—*Richard Foster*

That's another lesson in keeping moving forward, in never stopping. Action is the most important element of success. That sounds obvious, but so much stands between us and action. Most of what stands between us and action is our rational selves. It doesn't make any sense to believe, to take the leap of faith, and yet we must.

It's me who is standing between the old me and the new me.

The sooner we realize this, the sooner we are compelled to act. To take that leap of faith.

The End?

We think of making a definitive act, a daring act, as the end of our journey. We did it! We found our purpose, we resolved to act, we made a plan, and then we took the leap!

This is all excellent. This deserves celebration and reward.

But achieving our purpose in life requires that now that we're on our path, we stay on it. This is not as easy as it sounds. The good news is that there are rules and tricks to keep you moving forward that we'll discuss in the next chapter.

The end is in sight.

Don't even think of stopping now.

6

STAYING FOCUSED IS THE KEY

How to Achieve Your Purpose

Step 4: The Secret of Perseverance

Success is not due to talent, not title, not money, not wealth, not looks: it's the ability to work hard for a long period of time toward a goal.

I told you the story of when I got Scarlet Fever in third grade. I failed 3A for missing too much school. All my friends went on to 4B, but I was stuck. So what did I do? I didn't just go to summer school; I attacked summer school. I rode my bike there every single day and worked harder than I'd ever worked before. Eight-year-old me had a specific goal: to catch back up to my friends, no matter what. My mother was a working single mother. My grandmother and my aunt also had full-time jobs. No worries—I had perseverance. I rode my bike back and forth in the

Detroit heat, passing my friends playing ball in the park or eating ice cream under shady trees. Nothing stopped me. Soon, I found I loved learning. I had developed a passion. If I got stuck, I asked for help. My aunt, a teacher, got me tutors. My grandmother and sisters stepped in to help.

By the end of the summer, I was not only caught back up with the other kids, I had developed a whole new love of learning.

Researcher Angela Duckworth, the founder and CEO of CharacterLab, would say that I had grit. I wasn't smarter than the other kids. I didn't have more money. It certainly wasn't my looks. What I did have was a specific goal and the stick-to-it-ness required to achieve that goal. In other words, grit.

Grit is a combination of passion and perseverance for a singularly important goal. It is the hallmark of high achievers in every domain.
—*Andrea Duckworth*

Notice that grit has three components:
- Passion: I really wanted to keep up with my friends.
- Perseverance: I kept at it, despite the heat, the work, and missing out on the fun.
- A singular goal: I had to pass 3A to get to 4B.

If any of these elements was missing, I wouldn't succeed. When all of these elements were present, I was on the path to victory. Grit, according to Duckworth, is the number one predictor of success.

When One Item Is Missing

When I decided I couldn't be a minister in the church because I wasn't perfect, I no longer saw a goal for myself in the church. I still loved God with passion. I still prayed and worshipped every Sunday, with perseverance. But because I didn't have a goal, I was stuck. Nothing was achieved. I didn't move forward. I wandered. Only when I came back after four years to set my goal to become a leader in the church did my life begin to change, and I began to grow.

When I resigned from Coca-Cola Enterprises, Inc. and went to Atlanta to work for Frito-Lay, I started with passion, perseverance, and a goal. I loved being back in Atlanta. But a year into my work with Frito-Lay, the company changed course and decided not to expand in Atlanta by adding on a new facility for me to manage. Instead, they asked me to move to Kansas City, Kansas. I was single and needed the income, but I wasn't interested in going to Kansas City, far from my friends and family. I had, not too long ago, moved from Detroit to Atlanta. I wasn't thinking about moving again. So, I kept my place in Atlanta and moved to an apartment in Kansas City. That raised eyebrows. Was I really serious? If I was serious, then wouldn't I set up a real home in Kansas? Did I have the passion to keep working hard at Frito-Lay? In other words, did I really want this?

Around this time, I met a woman who would become my girlfriend and future wife. She was in D.C. My daughter at that time was in North Carolina. My friends were in Atlanta. I was not happy, spread all over the country, but I made the best of it. Why?

Because I had perseverance: I was always a hard worker, willing to stick to it.

But when I pictured the vision of my future in Kansas City, I couldn't stir up the passion for it.

When my daughter graduated in 2007, she decided she wanted to go to grad school at the University of Georgia. I told her to come back to Atlanta, and we'd live together. I left Frito-Lay. I had perseverance and a goal, but no passion for that goal, so I knew I wouldn't grow there.

The next option—having a goal and a passion but no perseverance—is the most common situation I see in those I love and those I lead.

Most people fail to achieve their goals because they're dreamers, not doers.

People say, *I'm gonna do this someday. If I win the lottery, if I get the promotion…* **if if if.** Instead of dreaming, you have to put your feet in motion.

I don't want to hear you say, *I want to.*

I want to hear you say, *I'm going to.*

Sacrifice, self-discipline, going the extra mile—this is what it means to persevere. Turn off the TV. Hold off on doing the fun things you want to do. Get to work!

Everyone wants to be wealthy, stronger, faster, richer, healthier, and happier. But those who achieve these goals do more than want. They hang in there and do the work, no matter how hard it is. At the end of the road is victory. Bored with your job? I encourage you to find something that you like to do so much that you would gladly do it for nothing. Then learn to do it so well that people would be happy to pay you for it.

Decide What One Word Will Describe You Next Year.

Maybe that word is *perseverance*.

Maybe it's *passion*.

Mine is *breakthrough*.

Often, people either don't act, or they try to grow by leaps and bounds and so give up because they've bitten off more than they could chew. But I've been at this for a while. I'm nearing the end of my path. This is the year I will cross the finish line—if I keep on displaying grit.

The Story of a New Kind of Mattress:

Bobby Trussell was a failed horse guy. He was deep in debt, with a wife and kids, and he didn't know where to turn. He started going to church, and he started to pray.

He founded an air ionizer company—and failed.

He dreamed up a 1-800 number geared toward horse betting—and failed.

Then, ready to give up, a friend offered him a business opportunity. He had a new product that had never been tried before in America: a foam mattress. If Trussell could sell 10,000 mattresses in the next year, his friend would give him exclusive North American rights to the product.

Trussell sold 70 mattresses.

Despite this, his friend stuck by him. (You can't do it alone!)

Trussell spent twelve years—twelve years!—trying to make foam mattresses work. All mattresses then were spring mattresses. Everyone thought he was nuts.

He called every chiropractor in the phone book, begging them to try his product.

He called the buyer at Brookstone every single day for weeks until finally, the man called him back to tell him to please stop calling. That was the opening Trussell had been waiting for. He begged the man to just take the sample he'd sent out of the box. The man did—and placed an order for 500.

After years of trying, Trussell had himself the hottest seller at Brookstone. Trussell's company was called Tempur-Pedic, and it would soon go public and earn Trussell millions of dollars. When asked if he thought he was smarter than other people, or a better businessman, Trussell said no, but he knew he was more perseverant. He kept at it even when others doubted him. Even when nothing was going right. And the reason he kept at it was that when he had been working with horses, he knew he wasn't really helping others. But he believed in his foam mattresses. He knew that they could help millions of people get better sleep. This gave him passion.

Passion. Perseverance. And a goal. This man had grit. Now, he had millions of dollars and was the CEO of a major company on the New York Stock Exchange.

I kept trying different things… I'm definitely not smarter than other people… I'm a risk taker. Perseverance combined with luck is what got me where I wanted to be.
—Bob Trussell to Guy Raz on NPR Radio,
How I Built This

- Starbucks didn't reach its fifth store until thirteen years into its history.
- Sam Walton didn't open his second Walmart store until seven years after starting his first.
- FedEx made its first profit in 1975, thirteen years after its founding.

The myth of overnight success is just that, a myth.
—Seth Godin

No One Can Run Their Race Alone

Life is a marathon. The first mile and the last are the easiest. It's the middle part where you struggle and want to give up. The good news is that this is where you meet people along the way. Other runners will say, "I'm with you, I've got you. We're going to make it together." Your legs ache, your whole body aches, you just don't feel you can make it. But the other runner says, "We can do it together.

I have brought people with me." Someone comes out of nowhere with a word of encouragement, and it makes all the difference.

Of course, you'll sometimes find yourself alone, waiting for others to appear. Still, you must persevere. You must stay focused. Then, you can use self-talk until the next helper comes along. You're tired. Everything is saying stop. But you say to yourself out loud, *I've just got a quarter mile to go. Keep going. Charles, you've got this.*

Sometimes, you've got to call your own name.

Grit in the Athletic World

My daughter was a sprinter. She was so fast—and I'm not just saying that because I'm her father! One day she was racing, and she slipped and fell. There was no way she was going to win that race. But she got up anyway. She was determined. She knew that she wasn't going to win, but she was going to finish. Sure, she was disappointed. But she wasn't going to lay down and cry.

No matter what—you fall, you detour—you get back up, you get back on track. Not just for yourself, but because it shows other people how not to give up, either. People saw her get back up and run. She became a person of inspiration and motivation and a model to others of never giving up.

One afternoon, I went to a meet to watch my daughter run, and there was a long-distance race going on at the same time. Many had finished the race and had crossed the finish line long ago. But the crowd was still cheering for those still running: *Come on, you can do it.* There was a person who was in last place, but who cares? They didn't give up. They crossed that finish line. They made it.

And that inspired others to say to themselves, *there's always a next time. I have to keep on trying. One day, I'll win this race if I just stay in it and persevere.*

- Pat Summitt, Tennessee Lady Volunteers Basketball Head Coach, didn't win her first championship until her thirteenth year of coaching.
- Dabo Swinney, Clemson Head Football Coach, lost fifteen of his first 34 games. He thought he was going to be fired. In fact, he was on the verge of getting fired, and then he won his first national championship.
- John Wooden, UCLA Head Basketball Coach, won his first national title in his sixteenth season.

Life is a Parade

The Thanksgiving Day parade started marching down Woodward Avenue in Detroit in 1924. It was sponsored by J.L. Hudson's, Detroit's most famous department store. At the end of the parade, Santa Claus would step from his float and accept the key of the city to the cheers of thousands of children like myself who were sure he was absolutely the real Sana Claus. Every year, I'd watch that parade go by, waiting to see Santa. It was worth waiting, because seeing Santa was such a reward.

Life is like that Thanksgiving parade, only you're not watching, you're the one marching down the avenue. You're a child, then an adult, then a husband, a father. What is at the end? What are you marching towards? Along the way, you have joys and sorrows.

Sometimes, you want to stop right there in the middle of the street.

You can't stop.

You must have grit.

That parade is going somewhere.

Where is your parade going?

At the end of my route, I want to be empty. I want to have given everything away along the way. I want the people I marched with, and the people who watched me march, to remember what I'd given them. I want to have made an impression, to have left a legacy. In the Detroit Thanksgiving parade, the marchers would throw candy to the crowd. I wanted to throw everything I'd learned in my life back to the crowd. All that I've been given, give it back.

I had a goal: to reach the end of that parade with no regrets, nothing weighing me down.

I had perseverance: rain, snow, sleet—no matter. No one could ruin my parade.

I had passion: I love the march. I love giving of myself for others' joy.

What is your goal? Your passion? Do you have the perseverance to carry on?

The Pool of Bethesda

It's alright to hold a pity party. It's OK to stall. Just so long as you start the motor up again.

You have to look behind the music and the flash. Someone else may be successful today, or they may look like they're going nowhere. Everyone is on their own journey. Keep your eyes on your own prize.

The story of the Pool of Bethesda is a good one when you're feeling that you don't have the perseverance to keep going. It's about a man who cannot walk. He is waiting by a pool that is supposed to grant miraculous powers to the first person into the pool, when the angels "stir the water." But every time the waters rise or fall, the man cannot reach the water fast enough. For 38 years, he'd been ill, searching for a cure. When Jesus comes to the side of the pool, he doesn't carry the man into the pool. He doesn't give the man an empty pep talk. Instead, he tells the man to get up and walk.

The man does so.

It's a miracle, but a miracle that forced the man to take the first step. He had to act. No one is going to carry you on your journey. No one is even going to get out of the way. But you must crawl, hop, jump, run, whatever you've gotta do to lift yourself up, even if for 38 years, you haven't been able to.

Believing you can do it is half the battle. Whatever the mind can perceive, it can achieve.

Doing it—actually acting!—is the only solution.

You keep on trying for as long as you have to try.

That's grit. That's the secret of success.

- Grit is the ability to work hard for a long period of time towards a goal.
- Grit allows you to move forward in the face of failure and rejection and obstacles.

- As we make our way along life's journey, nothing will be given to us. We have to work for it. We have to persevere, overcome.
- Grit keeps you moving forward.
- When life knocks you down, true grit won't let you quit.
- Stick with what you've got going, and see it through to the very end.
- Don't take your eyes off the prize. Stay focused and reach your goals.
- Success doesn't happen overnight. Anything worthwhile takes time to accomplish.

***You can choose the pain of discipline and sacrifice
or the pain of regret.***

Grit in the Corporate World

In my corporate work, I lead teams to meet and exceed goals. I need to keep focus not only for myself, but for the good of the team. I tell my team:

- When we focus we win.
- When you focus you win.
- When we all focus we all win.

This is grit for teams. Everyone plays a part. When we focus on growing ourselves and then adding our own individual passion and goals, we make for a better community.

The #1 predictor of success is perseverance and patience to reach long-term goals.

—*Angela Duckworth*

7

DELAYED BUT NOT DENIED

External Roadblocks and How to Overcome Them

The pessimist complains about the wind. The optimist expects it to change. The leader adjusts the sails.

—*John C. Maxwell*

We were living in Detroit when my wife received a promotion at her job with Kraft Foods in Atlanta. I decided to leave corporate America and pursue ministry and finish seminary. So we decided to take the leap of faith. We'd go together to Atlanta, and I'd leave the corporate world to start Go Tell It Ministries. I'd also be a stay-at-home dad to our then six-year-old daughter, who was going into first grade. Instead of being a leader and a manager of a company, I became a leader and a manager of a household. I was excited about that while I pursued the promise of my ministry.

I could have played it safe. Instead, I stepped out on my

own to my own ministry. For my first job outside corporate America, I could have accepted a pastoral appointment through my denomination. But I didn't want to be appointed to a location out of my control by a bishop or presiding elders. I wanted to start my own community where I saw fit, and that was in Atlanta, Georgia.

My vision was to form a teaching ministry. From Disciple to Discipler was the focusing concept of my studies and my intellectual energy. I wanted to create leaders who could expand to other locations and minister in their own communities. If I could create ten leaders, they could each then create ten leaders, and so on and so on. It would be the future of the church.

My wife never liked the idea of being a pastor's wife. She wasn't thrilled for it. She liked that I worked for Fortune 500 companies. She felt that I was taking a huge risk in starting a ministry of my own. I was sure she was wrong. I just knew it would be smooth, because I had the passion, perseverance, and a clear goal. That is, I had grit. I had an education: in the four years before, I had become a licensed minister, had been ordained as a deacon, then as an elder, and then had gotten my Master's in Religious Studies. I had a plan—more or less. Maybe not the best one, but an idea of where and how to start. And was I ever ready to take that leap of faith.

Part of the reason I was so eager may have been that my oldest sister, Deborah, had just passed away. It was a crucial moment in my life. After I saw her through her illness and preached her eulogy, I felt that time could run out at any moment. Life was short. I had stepped up in her illness to lead my family in mourning and recovery, and that had showed me that I had the potential to become a spiritual leader.

I was 34 years old.

Well, to make a long story short, my ministry didn't work out. My eyes were bigger than my stomach: I had bit off more than I could chew. It was a humbling experience. I cleaned house, and I got my daughter to and from school. But the ministry wasn't growing as quickly as I would have liked. It was a house not completed. I was embarrassed. If not now, when? It had to be now, I was sure of it.

And yet, that wasn't working out the way I had foreseen.

> *Those who dare to fail miserably can achieve greatly.*
> —*John F. Kennedy, Jr.*

What Went Wrong

When I look back, I thought things would happen automatically and quickly. But that's not how life works. I had to build one relationship at a time, with focus and perseverance. Instead, I was restless, watching my wife's corporate career build while mine was stalled, so I started a vending machine business.

Also, I started teaching marketing part-time at Clark Atlanta University. In addition, I took a job as a general manager at a Taco Bell. It did well, and soon I was managing a second store. It was hard, thankless work. You had to have a crew, and if you were short-handed, you stepped in yourself to do the work. This wasn't the vision I had in my head of my future. I was in an environment of semi-retired, part-time, college and high school kids just biding their time. Between the demanding work and assisting my wife in taking care of my daughter and the rest of our domestic affairs, I couldn't focus on my ministry.

Then, when a job opened at Coca-Cola Enterprises, Inc., I jumped on it.

In truth, neither I nor my family had been ready to leave corporate America and the prestige and security that it afforded. I had never focused. The time hadn't been right to put all my eggs in the ministry basket, and deep down, I knew that, and so I didn't. I was too committed to family and to living comfortably.

Fail Forward

One way to look at the situation was that I had failed. Another way was to say that I had leaped and landed—just not where I expected, but in a new place all the same, and that place was, although I didn't see it at the time, the right place for me to be.

With experience comes failure.

There is no surer rule in life. Failure can immobilize you, or it can take you to a new level. It gives you experiences that you can build on. It gives you opportunities that you can learn from. The important thing is that you learn from failure. When you fail, you don't give up. You get up. And then you move forward.

You can keep your journey moving, step by step, failure by

failure, just so long as every failure is learned from. Because an opportunity learned from is not a failure, it is movement forward.

> *Fail early, fail often, but always fail forward.*
> —*John C. Maxwell, Failing Forward*

No Just Means Not Yet

In chapter two, I told you the story of my going back to Coca-Cola. The moment that I realized my ministry was not going to work was the same moment I returned to Coca-Cola. As I explained previously, there is no way Coca-Cola should have hired me again after I had settled a wrongful termination lawsuit against them a decade or so before. But they not only re-hired me, they made me the training and development manager, and then they promoted me four times.

Coming back to Atlanta brought me back to a world-class corporation, stock-full of opportunities to grow and learn.

I believe God had a plan for me. He brought me to Atlanta on the dream of a ministry, and he kept me there to further prepare for that dream. I was impatient to get started, but it wasn't my time. Remember all those stories in the previous chapter, about how long it took many entrepreneurs to succeed? Five years, ten, twenty—they failed over and over, but never gave up. So whether you believe it's not your time because of God's plan, or because you're just not ready, or because the universe isn't yet in alignment, the important thing is to learn from your mistakes, and keep moving forward.

The difference between average people and achieving people is their perception of and response to… failure.

— *John C. Maxwell*

Abraham and Sarah

God promised Abraham and Sarah a child. But years passed, and none came. So Abraham and Sarah, impatient, got their young Egyptian slave girl, Hagar, to have a child with Abraham. They named that child Ishmael. Abraham thought, I'm 90 years old. I'm running out of time. He was desperate, and so he tried to manufacture something too soon. Sure enough, soon after, Abraham and Sarah had Isaac. The presence of Hagar and Ishmael caused friction in the household. By not waiting on God's timing, they made everything more complicated. Hagar and Ishmael were sent into the desert.

The story tells us that you have to wait on the Lord. God will deliver, but the conditions for Him to deliver lie in trust, hope, faith, and obedience. You need to come to a place where you understand that if God said it will be, it will be. But maybe the time isn't yet right. Little did I know, when I arrived in Atlanta, there were some things that God was going to work in me, and through me, and around me before He fulfilled his promise to me.

But you don't have to believe in God to get meaning from the story of Abraham and Sarah. One take-away is that no just means not yet. If you don't get bitter and keep on getting better, one day, your time will come.

You will fail. But you won't be judged by your mistakes, rather by what you've done to overcome your mistakes. Failure isn't our enemy. It's our partner in growth. It doesn't define you. It refines you. The path to greatness is never behind you. Just keep moving. Trust the process. When you keep doing things the right way, the numbers will rise, and the wins will come.

Human Time vs. the Universe's Time: The Story of Joseph and His Brothers

Joseph was only seventeen years old when his jealous brothers sold him to slaveholders and told their father that he was killed by a wild animal. Joseph made the best of his lot and worked hard as a slave for decades. But again, he was betrayed, this time by the wife of his master, who told her husband that Joseph wanted to lay with her. This wasn't true, but the master believed his wife and threw Joseph into an Egyptian jail. It's unclear how long he was in jail, but at some point, he was joined by one of the Pharaoh's servants. He interpreted the servant's dream correctly and begged the man to tell Pharaoh about him when he returned to Pharaoh's court. But for two years, the servant forgot about him. When he finally remembered, Joseph was released from prison in order to help Pharaoh interpret a mysterious dream. He correctly interpreted Pharaoh's dream, and finally was able, at 30 years old, to live a free life.

From seventeen to 30 is thirteen years. That is a long time to be a slave and to be in prison, through no fault of his own. What was God's reason for making Joseph suffer for no crime for so long? Even worse, he suffered for the evil and the forgetfulness of the people around him. Why? In other words, how do we explain it when we are forced to wait for our dreams to be fulfilled? Especially when we feel as if our waiting is filled with undeserved punishment?

Like Joseph, we must make good of the years God has given us to wait:

- **Joseph learned to be faithful:** before Joseph experienced his hardships, he acted as an informer for his father, betraying his brothers by telling his father if they did wrong. God must teach Joseph to be faithful to those around him, a crucial skill of a leader.
- **Joseph learned to serve:** before he experienced his hardships, Joseph's brothers worked in the fields while Joseph was favored by his father. Joseph allowed himself to be put above them. He had to learn to serve others before he could be a true leader.
- **He learned to be humble:** before he experienced hardships, Joseph proudly wore the fancy coat of many colors that his father had given him. A leader cannot be proud, and God was preparing Joseph to be a leader.
- **Joseph learned to be a doer, not a dreamer:** Joseph is literally a dreamer in the beginning of his story. He had dreams and told others about them. In order for Joseph to lead, he had to be a do-er. That is what he became, leading the Egyptians to store their great abundance.

What You Can Control and What you Cannot: The People Around You

Even if you respond positively to failure, sometimes the people around you won't. When you give some people a bouquet of roses, they say, beautiful. Others look at the bouquet of roses and say, *yeah, but… look at the thorns!* Sometimes you can avoid these sorts of negative thinkers. If so—then do! But other times, they're your family or maybe friends whom you otherwise value. Don't get mad at these people. Ignore them. Don't argue. Then, show them that you can do it. Believe me, when it's time to celebrate, they'll be there.

Critics can be inspiration. When people tell me no, I say to myself, I'll show you. Just wait and see. Let your light shine. Follow your dreams. Run toward them. Let naysayers be motivators.

> *Ignore the critics. Do the work. History doesn't remember the critic; it remembers the one who accomplishes the deed.*

For everyone who is negative, there will be another person who will be positive. Maybe you're down to your last dime, and by chance, a neighbor stops by with a pot of soup. You just have to believe. These people are out there, and they will reveal themselves when you least expect it. Often, it takes an emergency to bring people together. But they will come.

The Highway of Life

The highway is the road of your passion. It's God's path for you. Follow it, and you arrive at your purpose. Stay on that road, and you reach your destiny.

Every exit takes you onto the road of temptation. This is the devil's path. Follow it, and you can be lost for decades. You must get back on the main highway.

The highway is good. The exits are bad. Sometimes you know what you're doing when you follow the signs to an exit, but you don't listen. Curiosity killed the cat. Sometimes, you're just not paying attention, and before you know it, it's too late to merge back onto the right road. There are times when you're forced off the highway, because there's too much traffic, or an accident, or maybe even because the road closes down.

The important thing is to always strive to get back on your path.

There can be good in a detour. Open your eyes to other possibilities. Explore. Learn life lessons. But it costs you something. Time, for sure. Maybe you run out of gas when you're wandering around on those back roads. As you search for a way back, ask yourself: what did you learn from your exploring?

The Story of Home Depot

Bernie Marcus and Arthur Blank were perfectly happy, on the road to a comfortable life and respectable success. They were both executives at Handy Dan, a perfectly good home improvement store in Southern California. When Handy Dan's parent company was bought out by venture capitalists, Marcus and Blank were sure that they were safe. After all, Handy Dan was making a lot of money. It didn't make sense to fire its executives.

And yet, both men were given the ax.

They had thought that they were on the right road, until they were blindsided by a venture capital firm speeding past. But this tragedy turned out to be the best thing that ever happened to them. Getting stopped on their road opened their eyes to the fact that the road on which they were traveling was actually a detour.

Sometimes, what looks like a disaster is the universe telling you it's time to grow.

Marcus and Blank had a passion for the industry. They had been experimenting with price at Handy Dan and had recently discovered that if they marked down products, sales increased, and thus cost as a percentage of sales decreased. What if they could open huge stores, with marked-down prices, huge sales, and low costs?

At first, it was a complete failure. They opened huge warehouse stores that offered thousands of products at slashed prices. They kept the stores messy, to emphasize how just-the-basics their stores were.

But no one came in.

They sent employees and even their own family members onto the streets to give out dollar bills to spend in the store.

Even the free money didn't work. They had so little cash, they had to stock their shelves with empty boxes to pretend that they had inventory.

But eventually, through word of mouth, customers started showing up.

The new business model for home goods worked.

Both men became two of the most successful businessmen in the country.

There are no wasted souls. There is no wasted failure.

Look around you and decide: are you on the highway or on a detour?

Then get yourself back to where you belong.

And if there's something blocking your way, be watchful and learn from it. Your time will come.

The Top Five Reasons People Don't Succeed

Besides the time not being right, there are other reasons that people don't succeed:

1. **Lack of perseverance.** Don't stop now! Keep going. The only way to be sure of failure is to not even try.
2. **They have no education.** Their lack of preparation always shows. You must know your business and your customers' needs. Educate yourself before you act!
3. **Lack of curiosity.** You must constantly ask questions. I ask the people I supervise to tell me what success looks like in your mind. Tell me what being the best salesperson means to you. How do you think you can get there? What can you do?

4. **Perfectionism.** I once watched a person I was supervising build a Christmas-themed display. She built it, tweaked it, changed it, and then changed it again. I coached her to keep moving. Sometimes, these people are too overwhelmed to take in the big picture, so they focus on the small things. They need to understand what is important now vs. everything. Break it into chunks, then be sure not to get stuck looking at the trees, when they need to see the forest.

5. **Lack of planning.** Organization and multitasking are critical to success. Life is a three-ring circus: your job, your family, and your community. You have to be able to balance the three, and you can't do that without a plan.

8

DON'T BE YOUR OWN WORST ENEMY

How to Learn and Grow from Your Mistakes

The greatest mistake we make is living in fear that we will make one.
— *John C. Maxwell*

Sometimes, the world stands in our way. Sometimes, we stand in our own way. We become our own worst enemy. We make mistakes, we fail, and we have no one to blame but ourselves. When we're faced with these sorts of situations, the last thing we can do is give up. These are the perfect opportunities to look closely at ourselves and our actions and decide how we will improve them moving forward. Look at this as positive. When the world stands in our way, sometimes there's nothing we can do but wait. When the obstacle is internal, there's no limit to the improvements we can make in ourselves and in our behavior.

Marriage/Divorce

A year after my daughter graduated from high school, my wife and I separated. She left me because I hadn't been faithful. I knew that I had made a terrible mistake. I confessed. I begged. She wanted to hear none of it. She had had enough after 23 years.

It was July of 2004 when I received divorce papers. I was 47 years old. I refused to sign them. I thought I could win her back. I thought I could make it right.

But I couldn't see that she had moved on without me.

This was a low point in my life. My career was down the tubes. My marriage was over. My daughter had left for college, which was great, but it left a huge hole in my heart and in my home. I contemplated suicide. But my daughter needed her dad, and that held me to not doing something stupid. Still, it was bad. I had never been so low. Usually, when something had gone wrong in my life, I found ways to look on the bright side. But this—I thought that there was no bright side.

I loved my wife.

And I had done her wrong.

I was not happy with myself looking in the mirror.

How could I ever fix a thing like that? Especially when she had no desire to fix it—not that I could blame her for that. I had to man up and accept my own responsibility.

The only good news was that I was prepared for hardship. I had been through so many tests by this stage of my life that I knew how to find help.

Asking for forgiveness is not enough. Action is not enough. Dedication must follow.

Time to Talk

The first step was to reach out to others.

First, I reached out to friends. These were the people who would support me without judgement, who would accept me with all my shortcomings. I needed listening ears. My friends played that role. I told them I knew I wasn't worthy. I was open, vulnerable, and sharing.

After they had listened, they offered words of wisdom and encouragement.

But what if I hadn't had friends? What if I had found myself alone, as people often do? One answer is to reach out to God. Pray. He will always listen and send someone your way.

But what if you also don't have God in your life? Then open your heart to the universe. When you make yourself vulnerable, your energy will attract people to you. Look for these people. They're out there.

And if you don't believe in the power of the universe either, remember that you are part of humanity. Every human messes up: this is what it means to be human. So look to those around you, and reach out. It's easy to think that others won't understand our pain or our failures, but they do, because they have been there themselves.

Next, I talked with my spiritual mother, Mother Stewart, my mentor. I poured my heart out. This is when the healing truly began. The veil began to lift from my eyes, and I began to truly see the error of my ways.

I apologized to my wife, but only out of selfishness for what I wanted. I wanted her back. I wanted our marriage back. It was still about me and my desires. I hadn't felt the true weight and consequences of my actions on her. I thought that to confess and apologize was all that was needed. But the hurt was too deep. I needed to do more.

I had to say to myself: this is a pattern, and I'm not going to act this way anymore. My wife saw that I was not following through. She was hurt.

So while the first step was to ask for forgiveness, action must follow. And after action, perseverance.

The difficulty of the situation drove me into depression. I knew I was better than the way I was acting. But knowing that did no good. The damage was done. And it seemed I couldn't stop my behavior. My daughter was watching her father behave badly, while I should have lived and breathed to be her role model. I had promised to uphold scripture. But I had gone against scripture.

I felt like a hypocrite.

I felt like a failure.

Over and over, I had to remind myself: I was a human being. I had to remember the cardinal rule of life: making mistakes is inevitable. I could beat myself up, or I could lift myself up.

You can't do over, but you can do better.

Time to Act

I realized that I could never bring my life back to what it was. I had hurt my wife too badly. I had to own the failure of my marriage and move on. I couldn't depend on my wife to forgive and forget. It wasn't her job to fix me or make me whole again. The only person who could pull myself out of the darkness was me.

After I had talked this all over with my friends and mentors, I no longer needed encouragement and love; I needed the challenge to improve my behavior. It was time to talk to professionals. I needed to change myself if I was ever going to become the person I strived to be.

One reason God created time was so that there would be a place to bury the failures of the past.

—*James Long*

Breaking Habits

I learned that breaking a bad habit is a process. Very few people can go cold turkey. You're blessed if you can smoke cigarettes for years, then decide it's over and never light another one. For most people, it's an up-and-down cycle. One step forward, two steps back. I became prayerful. I vowed to learn from my mistakes.

I learned that some streets you walk down, at the end, there's nothing but trouble. It is necessary to get off those streets. You need a new path. You need to get back on your true highway. And if you can't get off the street, then you need to prepare in advance for what you'll do when you get to the end.

There are no bad people.
There are only people with bad habits.

As a child, I faced verbal abuse from my stepdad when he would drink. As I got older, praying, inspirational music, working out, playing sports, and reading served as positive forces to counteract the negativity.

Whatever is holding you back, you need a plan. We can make plans to achieve our life's purpose, and we also must make plans to stop our damaging habits.

I love watching *My 600-Pound Life*, a reality television show about obese people trying to lose weight. These people pressed forward and achieved. They had self-discipline and a plan, which led to positive results. They had been bedridden, now they could function. It wasn't easy, but with a plan, they struggled through. We watch their victory, and we cheer them on. We like and admire people who strive to better themselves.

They pushed just a little farther each day. One more mile. One more push-up. One more crunch. And slowly, step-by-step, they achieved their goals.

Don't give up on yourself.

Be one of those people.

No matter what you've done, people will show up to cheer you on.

Talk Never Stops

I made a plan of action on what to do when temptation called. I took the leap of faith that I could be a better person, even if I was alone and suffering and had no proof that this was so. And then, with great grit and determination, I followed through on my plan.

I had become a better, worthy man. It wasn't easy, and it took time, but I had started low and risen high.

Later, someone called me out of the blue and asked me to do premarital counseling with couples. When I divorced, I had stopped doing this sort of work. What did I have to offer other people about how to have a successful marriage when mine had failed so completely?

I said I'd have to pray about that.

I did, and I was released to do it.

I had forgotten the lesson that had taken me years to learn before, when I thought I was too imperfect to be a minister: you don't have to be perfect to serve others.

I knew I had to be transparent: so I told the couple that I was there to learn, because I had also failed. I vowed to be vulnerable. It was hard, but I always prided myself on being an honest person, and now was not the time to stop. I couldn't keep my troubles inside. People aren't perfect, I counseled. But we must hold one another accountable, and we must believe, with God's help, that we all have the power to change ourselves and our lives.

By the end of the counseling, we all had mutual respect for one another. God ministered to me as well as to the couple.

The Best Ending

In the beginning, I thought that I wanted my ex-wife and my marriage back. And I did. But like all things in life, sometimes God has another plan. Now, several years later, I have no ill feelings towards my ex-wife or towards myself. If I won the lottery right now, I'd write my ex-wife a check for a million dollars.

This, truly, is an outcome worth savoring. Through hardship, I learned to improve myself, to forgive myself, and to cherish the woman who taught me how to be a better man. Love is the best ending, no matter how it manifests.

We must develop and maintain the capacity to forgive. He who is devoid of the power to forgive is devoid of the power to love. There is some good in the worst of us and some evil in the best of us. When we discover this, we are less prone to hate our enemies.

—Martin Luther King, Jr.

Lessons Learned

Being stuck. Suffering a near breakdown. Enduring depression. All of this can lead to breakthroughs. But to achieve a personal or professional breakthrough after personal failure, you must:

- **Own up to it.** Don't blame others for your mistakes. When the errors come from inside you, you must embrace them. It's the only way to move forward and to change. Hold yourself accountable. Instead of live and learn, learn and live.

118

- **Know the difference between forgiveness and restitution.** You can throw a rock through a window and say, "Sorry." But restitution is replacing the window. Emotional impacts can cost, and you must do everything in your power to repay for the damage you have done, both to yourself and to other people.
- **Get help.** When I entered my depression, all I wanted was to lay in bed and stay in the dark. I couldn't move. I didn't feel like doing anything. I knew I had to reach out. It was prayer and talk therapy that healed me.

I talked it through with others. You must trust people. You can't be timid about sharing with others. Many people feel that they don't have a community. This is not true. These people have just not reached out. If you reach out, you will find helpers. Or rather, they will find you.

I had a cousin. She was smart, a professional, married to a lawyer. She committed suicide over a failed marriage. If she had reached out to me, I'd have told her that there was so much more in her life for her. She had a son. She had family that loved her. But I didn't know, because she didn't reach out. I missed the signs. People ask for help in different ways. Maybe there had been some sign someone could have picked up on, some indication that something was wrong. But she kept it all well-hidden. People who commit suicide think they have no community. They are wrong. We are all a community of mankind. If I had known, I would have said to my cousin, "I'm here for you. I'm listening. I'm a good starting point. I can walk with you."

Those simple words, perhaps, would have been the first steps to pull her out of her darkness.

- **Be true to yourself.** When you're stuck, and fighting against yourself, you can't sit back and wonder, *why aren't I getting there?* You need to face the dark side. Everyone has one. Why do you think you wouldn't?
- **Stick it out.** We experience things not to kill us, but to teach us. Life moments make us better. They change our perspective. You're never the first one to make the mistake you made, and you won't be the last.

> *To move forward today, you must say goodbye to yesterday's hurts and tragedies.*

You Made It: Now What?

Remember way back in the introduction to this book, I told you that to find and follow your purpose is not enough? You must also help others find their purpose. You must lead them.

This idea is very strange for a lot of people.

Many people think that they're not leaders.

They think, *Who would ever follow me?*

But we must not only achieve our own goals, we must help others achieve theirs—and in the next few chapters, I will tell you why.

For now, I will give you one simple reason we must help others:

no one achieves their purpose on their own. Everyone along the way needs help and guidance. While you're on the way up, you believe that you have nothing to offer others, or that you did it on your own. But this is never true. Every successful person, whether they are aware of it or not, has reached up, out, and down. There is always someone above you, next to you, and behind you on the journey. If we only walk with the aim of raising ourselves up, then who are we to accept the help of others? When we reach our goal, will we celebrate alone? Is that ever a celebration, one man, alone? Instead, form a web of helpers and help-ees.

When you look around you, you will find that you have gifts to give others just as others have gifts to give you. Iron sharpens iron. A fulfilled life is a constant trading of knowledge and aide.

This idea will enrich your life tenfold if you embrace it.

Although your path is uniquely yours, you are not on it alone.

The next part of the book is the most important. It is what separates those who find and strive for their purpose from those who truly achieve their purpose.

Don't stop now!

Just when you think you've reached the end of your journey, you open your eyes, and you see that you have only just begun.

PART II:

YOU CHANGED YOURSELF, NOW CHANGE THE WORLD

9

WHAT GOT US HERE
WON'T GET US THERE

Why Leadership Matters for Everyone. Yes, Even You!

When leadership calls, you must listen.

My mother was born in Jacksonville, Florida. Soon after, she and her two siblings were abandoned by their parents.

Luckily, my mother's aunt and uncle took in my mother and her sister. Her brother was taken in by another relative. My uncle was a preacher, so my mother was brought up in the church, although she never became very religious.

Because her uncle was a presiding elder who oversaw several churches, he moved a lot for the church denomination, so my mother had to move, too. My mother loved her music, loved laughing, loved the gatherings of family and friends. She lived for the now, the present. She loved everyone and found the good in everybody.

Don't judge each day by the harvest you reap, but by the seeds that you plant.

—*Robert L. Stevenson*

As an adult, she never stopped bringing people together. She celebrated birthdays, anniversaries, and Thanksgiving. Christmas was her favorite holiday. Whatever excuse she could find for good food, fun, and bringing together interesting and colorful people was good enough for a party. She'd invite in total strangers, anyone, with no judgment. She'd put a big old pot of spaghetti on the stove and watch the All Star game or the Super Bowl. I can remember growing up, there would always be a clean-up committee before and after, and I was always on it. I didn't like that part much, but I was okay having all the people around. I was raised by a village. I think that's why I still love being around people and why I always see the positive in everyone and in every situation. It's in my blood.

Just before my mother passed, the mantle fell on me to take over the celebration responsibility, and I did so with gusto and gratitude. We still celebrate all the time. Even at work, I am sure to celebrate every victory, no matter how small. I will always be grateful to my mother for that gift.

Leadership is influence. Nothing more and nothing less.

—*John C. Maxwell*

My mother was married at the age of eighteen to my father, who was only 21. They quickly had four kids in a row. Suddenly, she found herself at 24 years old with four children. I was the last, born in Detroit on a cold December day, 1957.

My father was in the army when my first two siblings were born, so we lived on the base. My mother became a homemaker.

When I was five years old, my parents called a family meeting to tell us they were getting divorced. My sisters were ten, nine, and seven.

"Let's take a vote," my parents said. They asked, "Who wants to go with mom, and who with dad?"

This wasn't exemplary leadership. But they had been in a troubled marriage, and things had gone south fast. No one was thinking straight.

Don't thrust people into a leadership role they're not ready for. Autocratic style has its place.

The vote was three to one. Me and two of my sisters stayed with my mother. My oldest sister, Deb, went with my dad. It didn't take long until Deb came back to join us.

My mother found part-time work at Hudson's Department Store, but it was never a career. She was a single mother with four young kids, so she did what she could.

We are positive, not because life is easy. We are positive because life can be hard.

—Jon Gordon

A Mother's Management Strategy

My mother assigned the two oldest of her children to watch the two youngest. One older sister, Deb, was in charge of my youngest sister, Georgia. The other, Diane, watched over me. I didn't understand at the time that my mother was demonstrating transformational leadership: the ability to bring others up to not be followers, but to also be leaders in their own right. My sisters were learning to lead us. And we were learning how to lead ourselves.

You can't escape leadership. Even if you don't lead others, you lead yourself, and being able to lead others begins with leading yourself well. You can't reproduce what you don't have: self-discipline, planning, multitasking, positivity.

We were all extremely independent. By six years old, I was washing and ironing my own clothes. I organized my clothes by color, military-style. When we went to the grocery store, I made sure the food was organized on the belt for the cashier. I was proud of what I could do.

A good leader takes care of those in their charge. A bad leader takes charge of those in their care.
—Simon Sinek

When I turned nine, my mother sent me to live with my grandmother and my aunt. She knew I needed help at the time for being a hyperactive kid. My grandmother was a realtor. My aunt was a school administrator. They lived on the other side of town. Now, I was the man of the house. My aunt had two children, but they were older, away at college.

My grandmother worked hard: she got up with the chickens, did yard work, then when it was time to stop working at home, she went to work. If I didn't have school, she'd take me to her office with her. I went everywhere with my grandmother, including to church every Sunday.

You can lead a family. Lead one person.
If you have poured into someone, you are a leader.

Our neighbors and our best friends' parents also acted as parents for us. They would all always treat us as their own. In this way, I learned from everyone around me.

My grandmother believed that I should be a hard worker like her. I had chores at home, then a day of school, then after school was Bible study. I learned about discipline and having a work ethic. To this day, I'm a stickler for promptness. If a meeting is at seven, we're getting started at seven o'clock on the dot. That's just how I was raised.

Our community in Detroit was diverse—white, black, and Jewish. Everyone lived together as neighbors and friends.

My mother had married a new husband. He was a good man, but he wasn't perfect. He was a drinker. And when he drank, he got verbally abusive. He had demons from being in Vietnam in the army and didn't have the help he needed to deal with his trauma. But he wasn't physically abusive, and so I was never afraid of him.

"You're not going to ever be anything," he'd tell me. I knew it wasn't true. I'd show him. But still, it stung.

The problem with drinkers is that they're two-faced. There's the drinking person and the good person. We'd play catch, hit balls, go to baseball games. But he had sorrows.

Now, my motto is simple:

*No matter the person and what they've done,
just love the hell out of them.*

Never match negativity with negativity. Just continue to do positive, and it'll come back to you. One positive aspect of knowing my stepfather was that I never drank. I didn't want any part of it. You always have to take away something good from every situation.

Much later, my stepfather would come to hear me preach. He was touched and moved. He was a good man deep down, and I always tried to see that side of him.

*You have a choice: make life great or be sad or
depressed.
Get better. Do better. Make a difference. Be a positive
change agent, in your own life and in the lives of others.*

Leadership and Your Unique Purpose in Life

Just as everyone's past contains stories of leadership, everyone's present is also a story of leadership. Who is helping you toward achieving success? Who is accompanying you, standing by you on your journey? Who are you raising up as your follower? Who are you forming into a leader in his or her own right? Whatever your purpose, you lead, and you are led. You cannot do it alone.

One more time: you cannot do it alone.

> *No matter your goal,*
> *you need other people to lead and inspire you.*
> *But this is not all.*
> *You also need people to walk beside you.*
> *And, as I will explain later, you need to lead others.*

These three directions of leadership, up, across, and down, appear everywhere in your family history, your work history, and in your quest to fulfill your purpose. All three directions must be practiced in order for you to achieve your true purpose in your life and in your career. The earlier you see this, the sooner you will achieve your purpose.

But leadership, just like everything else on your journey, is not easy. You need to learn how to lead the same way you needed to learn the other skills required to attain your purpose. In the first half of this book, I taught you how to find and achieve your purpose. Now, I will teach you how to enact transformational leadership— the ability to lead others and make them into leaders, themselves.

Becoming a leader follows the same model as learning how to achieve your purpose: you need education, a plan, a leap of faith, and perseverance.

Who You Lead and How You Lead, Not If You Lead

You cannot choose whether to be a leader or not:
you are a leader.
The only choice you can make is
what kind of leader you will be.

As we see from the story of my life, we are all leaders in our families and our communities, whether we like it or not. My mother had limitations and weaknesses, but she was a strong leader. She sought help when she needed it, she reached out to others, and she brought a positive attitude to life, no matter the situation.

My father, my mother, and my step-father were all leaders in their own ways. Even in my father's absence, he led me to vow never to be absent from my own daughter's life. My stepfather showed me that despite a person's shortcomings, everyone still deserves to be loved.

No matter the question, love is the answer.

My grandmother and my aunt taught me that leadership and hard work go hand in hand.

Despite all the problems with the father figure/leaders I had known, I have kept in touch with all of them throughout my life. This was the positive side of my spirit, to love always, to lead always, because in truth, to lead is to love.

Leading is Influence

Look around your life and see who you are influencing right now, for good and for bad.

- Your children are watching you.
- Your siblings are watching you.
- Your parents are watching you.
- Your spouse is watching you.
- Your community is watching you.
- Your colleagues are watching you.

Thus, you are a leader. Choose to be a good leader. Then make someone else a leader, influence their life. Be aware of your influence. Embrace it. Do yourself proud.

Taking the Reins

My oldest sister, Deb, died at 37. Back then, families didn't talk about disease (Marfan Syndrome). I only found out later that she had an enlarged heart. They call it Abe Lincoln's disease: long fingers, too tall, and thin. She didn't like to be tall. She had to shop for special-sized shoes. But no one ever told me it was an illness until much later, when my second oldest sister told me.

Deb had a heart aneurysm. Before she died, December 1989, the day after Christmas, she made a big breakfast for the family. She went out of her way that Christmas in making sure it was a holiday to remember. Somehow, she knew that her end was near. By May, 1990, she was gone.

In April, before she passed, she came back from visiting her best friend in Los Angeles for a church revival. I was serving in the pulpit. Towards the end of the service, there was an altar call for those who wanted the minister to pray for them. I was compelled that night to come from around the pulpit and to go to where she was sitting. She looked aglow.

I said, "Deb, you need to go to the altar."

She did. One of the ministers prayed with her.

Do not be a spectator.
Even if you don't know why you're acting, act.
Even if you don't know why you're leading, lead.
The answers will come later.

On May 12, I was sitting for a final exam I had to write when my phone rang. It was my youngest sister. "Chip," (my nickname), "something is happening. Deb's in the hospital."

I told her, "Keep me in the loop."

While I was finishing writing my paper, Deb had to leave one hospital and go to another that specialized in heart surgery, because her chest pain was so bad.

My sister called back. "You need to come now."

I dropped what I was doing and went immediately to the hospital. Surgery was only going to give her a 50/50 chance. I called my father who lived in Fort Wayne, Indiana, some three hours away to let him know what was happening.

When I arrived at the hospital, my sister Georgia said, "Chip, Deb wants to see you."

Georgia stayed behind with my mother while I went into the room where they were prepping Deb for surgery. I grabbed her hand, and at that exact moment, Deb's eyes rolled to the back of her head, and the nurses started shouting, "Code blue!"

I got out of the doctor's way, telling my mom and sister, "Everything's fine," although I knew it wasn't. I went to the hospital chapel, where I was all alone. I knelt at the altar, and it felt as if God literally put a sock in my mouth. I couldn't speak. So I shut up and closed my eyes and lowered my head in silence. Then, I saw a vision of Deb in the bed and a cloud leaving her body. I heard an audible voice say, "Now, go and minister to your family, and I will minister to you later."

I went back to the hospital waiting room just as the chaplain arrived. He said, "She's gone."

A strength came over me. I had to go and tell my other sister, who had been in the hospital and was at home recovering. It was as if I had found in myself a supernatural ability: the ability to lead. I arranged the funeral. I did her eulogy. I committed her body to the ground. When I look back on those difficult days, I now understand that God's spirit, preparation, and passion allowed me, the baby brother, to step into the position to lead the family when they needed it most.

It's not the position that makes the leader, it's the leader that makes the position.

—*Stanley Hofftyn*

We never know who will step up to lead. A few months later, I had the urge to go to the cemetery. My daughter was five years old, and she asked, "Daddy, can I go too?" We drove to the cemetery and walked to the grave site. I had no words. We stood there together in silence, my daughter and I. As the tears rolled down my face, my daughter grabbed my hand and said, "Dad, everything is alright."

And she was right. She was leading me, her father, away from the darkness and toward the light. I dried my eyes, and everything was all right from then on. I'll never forget that day God ministered to me through my daughter.

Letting Leadership Happen

Twenty-seven years later, in the summer of 2017, my mother suffered a stroke. My sisters didn't tell me. They thought they were protecting me, because I was the furthest away and the baby of the family. I was 59 years old. I didn't need protecting, I needed to be included.

You cannot do it alone.
Family, friends, professionals, strangers, God.
You need to let others in and let them find their role.
Do not give in to silence and exclusion.
Always choose communication and inclusion.

During the last conversation I had with my mother, she said she wasn't doing well. I encouraged her to fight. In hindsight, she was at the end of her journey. She went into an assisted living facility in February, and by August, she had passed away.

I was happy that I had spoken to her and had visited her back in March for her birthday and then returned for Mother's Day. That was the last time I saw her. Just before I left her to head to the airport, we took a selfie. As I walked through the hallway to leave, something came over me, and I teared up. Little did I know that would be the last time I would see her alive.

From Family to Fortune 500

Look at your family, and look at your life. The kinds of leadership you've seen and experienced will influence the kind of leader you'll become. This can be a good thing, but it can also lead you astray. What got you through your life so far will not be enough to get you to the next level, which is achieving your true purpose. It also will not be enough to get you to the ultimate level, the level which maybe you haven't yet acknowledged is within you and within your grasp and which will truly transform your life: leading others to help them achieve their purpose.

We'll talk more about this in the next chapters.

I was able to step in and lead during my sister's death, because I had worked hard to be a leader in my religious and corporate education. But in truth, it took me many, many more years to become an effective leader in every situation I encountered. I still had a lot to learn. I believe that even now, I have a lot to learn.

Never stop learning to do. Never stop learning to lead.

Leaders are learners. According to John C. Maxwell, there are four phases of leadership growth:

1. **I don't know what I don't know.** As Maxwell points out, "As long as a person doesn't know what he doesn't know, he doesn't grow." This is the starting point. Many people will never move on from this stage. Do not allow yourself to be one of those people. Say to yourself: I must learn. Why? Because I have a purpose that I must achieve, and I cannot do it alone.

2. **What I don't know.** This second phase is often the most exciting. It allows you to open your eyes to the world around you and see how much there is to learn. Don't be discouraged. Take this as a motivating challenge: I can do it. Discovering what you need to learn is like discovering your purpose—it gives you a clear goal, and thus you now have a path for action. Having a plan, no matter how hard your plan, is always better than having no plan at all.

3. **Grow and know and it starts to show.** The time for hard work is now. You have a plan for action. You're fighting to succeed. But this is also the time for small triumphs. The more you know, the more you will move forward. Step by step, you will begin to transform yourself and your life. Remember to celebrate what you have achieved so far. Then keep moving. Don't stop now. The best is about to come.

4. **Simply go because of what I know.** You have your purpose. You have learned that you must lead to achieve your purpose. And now, you know how to lead. Everything is second nature to you now. You will still always be learning, but more and more, you will be teaching and raising others to their purpose. Nothing can stop you now.

In the next three chapters, we'll look at what we must learn about leadership so that we can influence the lives not just of ourselves, but of others. We need to be influencers, because on our own journey, we will constantly be in a position of leading, being led, and walking alongside. We cannot always be the follower.

Remember: no one can do it alone.

Open your eyes to others, open your heart. Bring them on your journey. Imagine them in front of you, beside you, behind you. Life is a parade. You must get off the sidelines and let it sweep you along in its power and its purpose. You are not walking alone down that street, with everyone watching you, waiting for you to perform, waiting for you to to wow them. You are with others. You are surrounded. You are protected. From them, you can gather strength, and you can give strength.

You can do this.

Stand up off the sideline.

Step into the flow of the parade of life.

Then move forward, always with an eye toward others around you.

The next three chapters will teach you how.

10

MY TIME, MY TURN

The Link Between Personal Growth and Leadership

When life was looking up in Atlanta, I was offered a promotion in Detroit—an executive position to manage a Sales Distribution Center for Coca-Cola Enterprises, Inc. What's ironic is that this was the same Sales Distribution Center that had closed down in 1987, when I'd been through the RIF (reduction in force). It was now reopened. This had been a real turning point in my life. When I think back to 1987, when I had gotten caught up in that reduction, I had thought that my career of being on the fast track had derailed. Now, I would come back and help run it. It felt like a sort of justice.

This move back to Detroit turned out to be a mistake. The Sales Center in Detroit had a strong union, and people weren't responding to my calls for change. I asked for another role, as I knew I wasn't succeeding in my current position. In hindsight, I had been trying to do too much, too soon. I hadn't yet learned how to be a true leader: that is, a transformational leader. At the time, I only knew it wasn't working, but I didn't know why.

In retrospect, I had taken the job for the wrong reasons: I had gone back to the scene of my layoff, and I wanted a kind of revenge. I wanted to show them they'd been wrong.

But also, I wasn't ready yet to lead the way I lead today. Back then, it was authoritative, my way or the highway. This was not true leadership, but I still had to learn.

One way I could have learned this lesson was to look around me in Detroit. I was in the perfect place to understand some of the most important lessons of leadership.

Leadership Lessons From the Field

Detroit was a blue-collar town. It had the big four sports: baseball, basketball, football, and hockey. I was ten years old in the summer of 1967, the summer of the Detroit riots and the year the Tigers lost the opportunity to go to the World Series by one game. I really got into baseball that year. Ernie Harwell, baseball hall of famer, was the announcer on the radio, and I listened to him whenever I could. I knew all the players, all the statistics, all the lineups. I only had one doubt in my mind: I wasn't sure if I would grow up to be a baseball player or a baseball announcer, but either one was fine with me.

The next year, the Tigers won the World Series. They would win it again in 1984. In 2004, the Detroit Pistons would win the National Basketball Championship. The Detroit Red Wings would win back-to-back Stanley Cups in 1996 and 1997 and two more in 2002 and 2008. And the Detroit Lions—well, there is a lot to learn from failure on the field as well as success.

If you want to understand the link between personal growth and leadership, a good place to start is to look to lessons from the athletic field.

Leadership Lessons from the Field #1: Knowledge

A baseball team has nine position players. Everyone on the team has a job, and they need the tools to perform their jobs. The infielders have smaller baseball gloves; the outfielders have bigger baseball gloves. They all have a role on the team, and they all have the responsibility to come together as one unit. The coaches at first and third base are on the sidelines. The manager in the dugout calls the plays to make sure everyone can succeed.

To achieve your purpose in life, you must build a team,
everyone with a role.
You fight to achieve your goal—to win—not for yourself,
but for everyone on the team.

Everyone who has ever been on a team knows that a good coach cares about everyone on the team. They do not want to win for themselves. They have the mindset of not leaving anyone behind:

- You cannot reach your purpose alone. You need a team.
- To lead that team, you need to be in it for everyone's sake, not your own.

- The selfish player or coach will never go far. They may win games, but they will never win championships. Be in it to win the championship—the ultimate prize, your purpose in life, and the joy of bringing others along on your way up to achieve their purpose, too.

How do you form a team? Players want to follow coaches with great talent, who have played the game. They want to follow people who have proven that they know how to win. If the coach isn't making the right choices, the players know. If they are free agents, they choose to go to another organization. It's not the city or the team or friends that make the team. Great players move to another club, because they're following a coach who knows how to get it done. The same is true with great companies. No one will stick with a bad boss even in a great company or a great city. People are always looking first and foremost for the leader who will raise them up.

They want a coach with knowledge. So the first step of leadership, just like the first step of achieving your purpose, is attaining knowledge. Take your time to gather the skills you need to move forward. Educate yourself.

- First, you educate yourself on your game, your goal, your purpose.
- Simultaneously, you educate yourself on how to be a successful leader, or you will never be able to achieve that purpose.

Ask yourself: why do some people emerge as leaders while others don't? The first rule of leadership, as Al Maguire, former head basketball coach at Marquette University observed, is that a team is an extension of the coach's personality. Leadership is personal, and it is about influence. In order to lead, you need to develop yourself in six vital areas:

- **Character:** who you are
  People will follow a person who is trustworthy, generous, and honest. If you show these traits, you will find people looking to you for leadership.

- **Relationships:** who you know
  People will follow a person who attracts good, positive people to them. Look at the people around you. Are these the sorts of people who will help you and others win? If not, then you need to find new people. Reach out. Reach down. Reach up. But only to positive, helpful people.

- **Knowledge:** what you know
  People will follow a person who has shown they know how to play the game, and they know how to win. This is the most basic trait of a leader. Are you that person? How can you become that person? Think about this all the time as you make decisions on how to spend your time.

- **Intuition:** what you feel
  People will follow a person who makes the right moves at the right time. This is following your gut, taking that leap of faith.

- **Experience:** where have you been, what have you done

  People will follow a person who has been there before. Get out there and do, do, do. The more you do, the more people will follow you.
- **Ability:** what can you do

  People will follow a person who is the best on the field. Focus on doing, not dreaming.

Begin to build knowledge of yourself in these six areas while you build knowledge of the game itself. Do you have these traits? What do you need to get them? How can you strengthen them? While you gain experience and knowledge by watching other players play, you must gain experience and knowledge watching others lead. Correct and change your behavior. Correct and change your thinking. In other words, you can't just learn all the traits of great players in the game you're playing, you need to learn the traits of great leadership in the game, too.

Leadership Lessons from the Field #2: Planning

Teams that are consistently growing and winning have strong coaching. Struggling teams are looking across the way at those successful teams. How can they get in on some of that magic? They may not be able to hire away the head coach, but they can poach the assistants. Those assistants can come over and work the same magic, because they have learned from their head coach what it takes to win. Take a look at the successful head coaches: there is a family tree of successful coaches that comes from their leadership and coaching.

If you're able to clearly articulate where you're going, which part everyone will play, and how you'll get there, you'll have put together a winning team.

When making a plan for your team, you need to have insight into your team's strengths and weaknesses as well as your opponents' strengths and weaknesses. You need to know your, and their, strategies and range of tactics. You'll need to understand everyone's role, including your own, and have a plan for everyone on the team to execute.

- The plan can be specific in the beginning, but then you can allow others to be creative. For example, in football, the quarterback must learn to run the set plays. Once he's demonstrated that he can get to the end zone and score with the set plays, then he can call an "audible." That is, he can go out on his own and become a secondary leader in his own right, on the field. So, you develop a plan, but then you also know when to let your team divert from the plan.

- In basketball, the point guard is the creative player. He or she also will learn the plays, but then go out on his or her own to execute it. They know how to distribute the ball. They know when to take over the game. They know when to shoot the ball. They also help the coach on the court. A great coach looks for these people who can be best of the best and help others along the way. They can provide leadership, not just act as a player.

- In baseball, the catcher is the one calling the plays and getting fielders into position. They have insights into what the hitters and pitchers can do. You give them a plan, but then you let them go out on their own to call their own game.

The magic of having a plan when you have a team is to watch your team take your plan and then run with it and make it even better.

This passing of plan from coach to player is called transformational leadership. We'll talk more about that later in this book, but for now, remember that it's the most important aspect of professional leadership.

Leadership Lessons from the Field #3: The Leap of Faith

I worked for The Hershey Company for twelve-plus years, and as I write these pages, I still do. So many lessons were learned, and throughout my career, I was promoted many times. At the beginning of my career, climbing the corporate ladder, I was in it for myself. What could I do to move forward? To raise myself up?

And then my career stalled. I tried for seven promotions at The Hershey Company and didn't get a single one.

This was when there was a shift in my thinking: a true leap of faith.

When I realized my company wasn't going to promote me, I began to look at my life and my leadership. There were many reasons, I believe, why I was not going to be promoted, and they were all out of my hands. I'm not going to discuss them in depth in this book, because they are not important here. This book is about positive affirmation and about moving forward, not looking backwards.

Be Better, not bitter.

This book is about your true purpose in life and the kind of leadership required to fulfill it. We all must choose what kinds of leaders we will be. What kinds of people we will be. We must choose whether we will pursue our true purpose in life, or continue on the path that isn't right for us. We may be doing good things but are not necessarily doing the right things.

I thought and prayed deeply on my situation.

I could wallow in my disappointment, or I could figure out how to thrive. I was making good money. I enjoyed my job leading my team. I've met some great and wonderful people in my career, but I've also met plenty of people with old mindsets. It's not racial, not bigotry, but rather just an old way of thinking that they're stuck in.

One day, a manager said to me, "Charles, I believe we've underserved you."

He was right. I was undervalued. I had so much education, so much experience. I knew that something was wrong there. But what was in their hearts was not important. What was important was what was in my heart. In my twenties, my thirties, I would have fought tooth and nail. I would have banged my head against that wall. I have fought my whole life against incredible odds to get where I was, but a voice was telling me that now, I had to fight a different fight.

> *If a man is called to be a street sweeper, he should sweep streets even as Michelangelo painted, or Beethoven composed music or Shakespeare wrote poetry. He should sweep streets so well that all the hosts of heaven and earth will pause to say, 'Here lived a great street sweeper who did his job well.'*
>
> *—Martin Luther King, Jr.*

It was time to take that leap of faith. Time to listen to that voice.

I saw it as clear as day. I had achieved everything at Hershey that I was meant to achieve for myself. I was where I was supposed to be. If this was the place that God had put me, he had put me there for a reason. I would coach and mentor my peers and those below me. I would encourage and support those beside me. As for looking for leadership above me—I had been looking in the wrong place.

Above me was one and only one mentor—God.

The corporate life is not my ultimate path. I was called to form a ministry, to bring my experience and knowledge to others, to inspire, motivate, and teach others not just in the corporate world, but in the spiritual and education world. I was put on this earth to lead others to their true purpose in life. For decades, I had been in it for myself—my promotion, my title, my salary—and I had built a successful and comfortable life. But now, I realized I was put here to serve others. The money, the power, and the prestige might sound good. Instead, though, I choose to give to others until I am empty.

This is my purpose in life.

I firmly believe that God has a plan for me that is for me alone. No one can block me if I follow his plan. I'm not envious or jealous of others, because their path is not my path. I work for a master, but people and corporations are not my master. I work for God—the real master, the only master. I report to the spirit of excellence. I know that in due season, I'll be taken care of. God has shown me my path. It's a spiritual message. Not corporate. Not political. I will take what I've earned and take what I've learned, and I will share it with the world.

It was humbling to realize that maybe everything wasn't about me—my promotion, my advancement—but what I could do for others.

I had discovered true leadership.

It was a revelation.

It was a leap of faith to accept and act on this revelation.

On my sixtieth birthday, my team bought me an Atlanta Braves jersey. On the back, it had the number 60, and my name, Redd. I wore it to the ballpark, and people asked me, "Who was Redd? When did he play? I don't remember him." I told them, "It's me," and we'd all have a good laugh. But it's more than a silly shirt; it's a metaphor for life. I'm a fan of the Braves, but I'm also a fan of what I bring to the table. I am never only a spectator in life. I am a player. I choose the game, and then I play it to the best of my abilities. I am an exemplary teammate and coach. I am here for the love of the game, the love of my team, and the love of God. I will never stop striving to win.

Leadership Lessons from the Field #4: Perseverance and Grit

I knew that this new area of play was not going to be easy. Easy would be to accept where I was and wait out my career. Easy would have been to lash out in anger and bitterness at things I couldn't change.

But this was not my way. I knew that I had a purpose to fulfill, and that now was the time. It is not enough to win the game. We must win the championship, go all the way. Don't let disappointments or setbacks lead you astray. Look to the big picture: you're not going to settle for anything less than achieving your purpose in life. Never, ever give up on your dreams.

Players win games. Teams win championships.

Whatever game you choose, you have to be in it for the long haul. You have to be in it for the grind, year after year, season after season. And you have to motivate others to join you in this difficult journey, because you cannot do it alone. You will not always succeed, but with grit, you will always move forward.

Success isn't permanent and failure isn't fatal.
—*Mike Ditka*

When I was young, I was taught that there's a time for everything. After school, I'd take off my school clothes, do my homework. I wanted to join the other kids playing outside, but I knew the homework would pay off to get the grades. I had to prioritize. Ask yourself: what's important now? Each and every day, it's a three-ring circus. Driving for results, making others around me better, and continuously learning and growing. I remind myself daily to stay focused on what's important and what must be accomplished.

People ask, *Am I fully committed to my work if I'm also pursuing my ministry? Am I fully committed to myself if I'm focused on helping others rise up?* The answer is yes and yes. I'm going to get an A in both classes. I will give it my all, taking time for each endeavor. I've always been a multitasker. I will work harder than most. I always have and will always continue to do so. But to be a winner, you must plan to win, prepare to win and expect to win.

Start each day by telling yourself: I am excited for the journey yet to come.

Every morning, the scoreboard is reset. You are given another chance to win.

Every day, the time sets back to zero, and you have the exact same number of minutes as everyone else to play your game.

Make the most of your opportunity.
On your marks, get set... go!

11

PUTTING YOUR BEST FOOT FORWARD

Different Kinds of Leaders and the Importance of Teamwork

He who thinks he leads, but has no followers, is only taking a walk.

—John C. Maxwell

Moses was the leader of the Jewish people. God chose him to lead them out of slavery in Egypt, and for 40 years through the desert toward the promised land. But God told Moses he would never see the promised land. Instead, God commanded Moses to teach Joshua to lead, because Joshua was the one chosen to lead the people into Canaan, the promised land. Moses suffered a consequence: he disobeyed God by drawing water from a rock by striking it instead of speaking to it as he was instructed. He had shown a lack of faith. But also, this was a necessary change in leadership. One sort of leadership was needed in the desert, to motivate and inspire the people to believe. But the crossing into the promised land would be a time of war, battle, and strife. This required another sort of leader for another sort of task.

Everyone has a role.

Identifying the best person to fill the role is one of the most important jobs of a leader.

Now that I had a clear vision of focusing on my job as a ministry and building my ministry as my next job, I had to consolidate my ideas of how to build and lead a successful team. This was a time of transition for me, but also a pause. It was a gift in which I could not only finish my corporate career on a high note of joy and giving back, but also study (knowledge!) and prepare (plan!) for the journey ahead (leap of faith!). First, I had to look back at what had worked in my leadership, and where I'd come up short.

The Autocratic Leader

Autocratic style has its place; for example, when I came into a turnaround situation at Hershey. I was starting a new job with a new team with half of the team being new to the company. Morale was low, and the team wasn't performing. This was a situation where I needed to take charge immediately:

I told my team that we were all going back to basic training. We needed rules, regulations, and procedures, and we needed to enforce these rules in a uniform manner. If everyone knew the rules, then there would be no excuses.

1. Here is the call procedure. Everything is scripted, down to where they should park their cars.

2. Here are the administrative duties and due dates: consistency and accountability is clear.

3. I went to the veteran leadership on the team and had one-on-one conversations to get their support and buy in. They'd be captains. But for now, they'd be assisting, enforcing my rules.

The team initially pushed back. They were used to doing what they wanted. They were used to expressing their opinions and complaining. But the autocratic style has no room for opinion. We were dealing only with facts. Now, no one could say, *It's not fair. Charles didn't like me.* The rules were the rules.

After balance was achieved, the shift could begin. I began to import—and export—talent. I could evaluate the results of each individual based on a level playing field. I could ask my teams: are we getting measurable results? But driving for results was only one part of success, because my secondary goal was making people better through positive leadership. I asked myself: are we getting our people recognized and promoted? This was a target that even the most cynical team member could buy into. They all saw that although I was an autocratic leader in the beginning, I wasn't in it for me, I was in it for them.

The autocratic leader needs to motivate the team in as many ways as possible. I had to instill in them what we stand for: a corporate culture.

No matter what kind of leader you are, motivation of the team is paramount. When you're an autocratic leader, you can tell your team that selling products is the goal. At Hershey, because we sold candy, we could also be motivated by saying that we put smiles on people's faces. But at Hershey, we had something extra in our culture: a school. Many years ago, Milton Hershey decided to use his fortune to build a school for 100 orphaned boys. Today, that school has grown into a co-educational school for boys and girls with over 2,000 economically disadvantaged students.

Now I am more interested than ever in maintaining and improving the morale and efficiency of all my companies.
I want to devote the rest of my life to that end, for the school.

—*Milton Hershey*

When we sell product, we're earning another scholarship for another child who wouldn't perhaps have the chance at a top-notch education otherwise. A corporate culture like this one makes it easy to stay motivated. If your corporate culture doesn't provide external motivation, look to the friendships you can form and the good you can do for your fellow employees. Always find the good that you can take away. You may meet the most important mentor or mentee in your life. The relationship stays. Always look to the positive.

The Transformational Leader

My goal was always to move from autocratic leadership to transformational leadership as quickly as possible.

Transformational leadership is leading with a mindset of creating other leaders, not followers.

As the team began to trust me, and I began to trust the team, I could be less hands-on and grant more empowerment to each team member. I wanted to convey that I respected everyone, and that everyone was needed. We were all operating on the same page. The old way was top-down. The new way was: the whole team made decisions, as individuals and as a group.

- Everyone could suggest things. They took ownership. They had earned the right to call their own plays.
- They could lead themselves. Each captain got their own piece of the pie. If there were 50 things we had to do as a team, I would hand off 30 of them to my captains. I became the conductor of the orchestra, assigning every section their own part to be responsible for based on their abilities and talents. If the music didn't sound right, I would intervene. If it sounded good, I would hum along, helping them keep their rhythm with the rest of the sections, then applauding when we were done.

For new managers, becoming a transformational leader, a positive leader, instead of an autocratic leader, is the most important shift they must make. In order to best shift the team, a leader must be aware of the leadership styles of the people he leads so that he can successfully make this shift from developing blind followers to developing motivated leaders:

1. **New Employees:** They need time to develop, whatever their type. They need a step-by-step performance plan and a lot of direct leadership. They mostly reach across to support one another.

2. **Professional Employees:** They've been with the company a while, but don't yet feel ready to rise. They can still be given leadership roles: they can be responsible for reaching down and supporting the newer employees and also reaching across to support one another.

3. **High Potential Employees:** These are the employees who do a great job from day one and want more. They compete for promotions and opportunities. They raise their hands. They have the executive disposition, business acumen, and the impact to bring others along. They look for leadership in life. They're clear on what they want to do.

These last kinds of employees are the joy and success of transformational leadership. The cream rises to the top. To identify these people who take initiative, I ask myself:

- Do their peers respect them as leaders on the team?
- Are they the point guards, the generals on the floor? Do they set others up for success, but also aren't afraid to take the winning shot themselves?

- At the dance, are they wallflowers? Or are they the ones who want to get out onto the dance floor and encourage others to join them out there.

Transformational Leadership in Practice: PPP Employees (Passion, Personality, and Professionalism)

When I was just starting out my career, a headhunter called me with a position in a tobacco company. Later, I was offered a job at an alcoholic beverage company. I didn't take either job. I knew I couldn't have passion working for these companies. I don't fault anyone who does this sort of work—everyone has their passions. But I don't smoke. I hardly ever drink. I have to be a part of what I sell. Hershey and the soft drink industry were perfect for me, because they were both very wholesome products. At Hershey, I can also believe in the Hershey School and its mission. Sales is always about chasing numbers and results. You have to really believe in what you're selling to turn a no into a yes. This is the first P: Passion.

Passion is what I look for when I'm looking for people with the capacity to rise up and lead.

The next thing that's needed is the second P: Personality. A leader has to be likeable and approachable. They have to be open, so that others feel safe and comfortable around them. They need to be able to be a butterfly: to fit into and out of all kinds of different social situations. They need not only to be able to talk, but also to listen. If you're not in the conversation, if no one knows who you are, then you're not going to be an effective leader.

When I first started out, I thought that my work would speak for itself. In the beginning, this is enough. But to progress, you have to speak for your work.

The third P is Professionalism. To be a leader, you must understand that you represent God and your company. You are an ambassador, an extension and reflection of those you serve. You must therefore display the character, attitude, and behavior of a professional.

The Fourth P

Many leadership theories stop with three P's, but I believe in a fourth. That is: Product Knowledge. What are you selling? You have to be great at fact-based selling as well as relationship selling. You need to know what's fair and bring that knowledge to your clients.

Reasons for Sub-par Leadership

The three—or four—P's are the reasons a leader succeeds. But it's also worthwhile to look at some reasons that a leader can fail:

- The employee who knows it all. They feel entitled and are sure that everyone else is wrong. This type of employee usually moves from one company to another, trying to find a situation that is as good as they are, but it doesn't exist, because they are so very, very good. This kind of employee has always been praised in their life before they've performed. They come from a culture where everyone on the team gets a jacket, gets a varsity letter, whether they truly played or not. You have to bust their bubble. You have to tell them: You've gotta try harder. You have to get better. Some will come to themselves. They want to be the best of the best. They're on social media: look at me! Others won't be able to listen. They'll usually leave the team on their own accord, looking for a place where their superior skills will be instantly praised.

- **The employee who doesn't do the job**. There are signs of an employee who isn't serious about their job, just merely going through the motions not adding any value to the customer and team. It's up to the leader to create a sense of community. These days, garages are separate from houses. You have to make an effort to come out and see your neighbors, play with the kids. Instead of pulling into the garage with no contact, a lost sense of community, you need to come out and walk around, shake hands, ask questions, and engage. It's the same way with modern companies. You need to make an effort to connect to your employees and allow them to connect with one another in order to keep everyone on track:

- **Face-to-face coaching.** No matter how far you are from your employees, you need to find opportunities for face-to-face meetings. Nothing truly substitutes for real human contact.

- **Face-to-face group settings.** It's not just about leader-to-follower interaction. The transformational leadership style requires the whole team to get together in order to support one another on every level.

- **Conference calls on Skype or other visual platforms.** Sometimes, it's impossible to get together face to face, and in that case, you still need to maintain human contact. How are they looking: Tired? Motivated? Distracted? You can reach in and raise up only if you can see and read human faces.

Birds of a feather want to flock together, but we must always stretch ourselves to learn from others who are unlike us.
The more experience we have with more types of people, the smarter we will grow.

I played basketball growing up with older kids. They beat me most of the time. I willed myself to compete. I pulled up to those who were already up. I moved to the highest level I could, even if I didn't feel ready. Be aware of opportunities to move outside your comfort zone, and act on them whenever you can. You just may learn something.

The Servant Leader

This is the ultimate goal of leadership. It's not about me at all, but about serving others. It's having the joy of caring for others. I understand the impact of my own attitude. I have a spirit of excellence that the team learned from the top, from my attitude. They know that whatever their current role, they must excel, because they see me thrive and be the best that I can be in my current role. I try to make the best of every situation; therefore they will, too. Instead of being for myself, for climbing the corporate ladder, I am for them. Now, they are also all for one another—and for me.

I had always been a servant leader in the spiritual community. Now, through bringing this leadership style to the corporate world, I prepare to build my next chapter. There is no difference between the church community and the corporate community. I want to become more and more like Christ, take on the process of yielding myself, buying into being a servant, not a master. This is how transformations occur. From the old to the new self.

Non-corporate Leadership: From Fortune 500 to Your Personal Future

When we lead in corporations, we often have a clear vision of what must be done, because it's handed down to us from the leadership levels above us. When we lead in life, what must be done is also handed down from above: it's our purpose. We look at our purpose in life, and from that, we extract our plan.

I say to myself, *Here are the ten things I must accomplish this year in order to achieve my purpose.* I put pressure on myself to multitask in life as I do in work:

1. Produce 100 podcasts on positive leadership
2. Become a certified trainer for Center of Teacher Excellence
3. Have a successful year with Hershey
4. Write five speeches
5. Write this book
6. Establish and execute a healthy food and exercise plan
7. Give five live audience speeches
8. Mentor five leaders
9. Celebrate life at every turn
10. Produce the weekly Redd line conference call

I know that this is too much to do this alone, so I built my team. People are part of every stage of it. I look to the kinds of people I bring in: what stage are they at in their leadership abilities? Are they new, foundational, or do they have PPP (passion, personality, and professionalism)? Are they motivated? By what? How can I motivate them further? How is their purpose part of my purpose? How can we aide one another? Everyone has something to offer. You have something to offer to everyone. Together, only together, can everyone reach their goals.

- What are your ten goals for your personal journey? How do they lead you toward your purpose? Make a list.

- Who can you bring along for the ride? Who can you reach out to in every direction: up, across, and down? Make a list.

Now, begin to assemble your team, with an eye toward moving everyone forward and lifting everyone up. Be positive, forward-thinking, and hardworking. In this way, you'll achieve your goals—and make your world a better place.

You will do it with others.

You will all change and grow together.

You will have a community around you and for you.

Already, your life has improved for the better.

Keep charging and changing toward your purpose.

12

FROM MOUNTAINTOP
TO MOUNTAINTOP

Passing the Mantle:
The True Meaning of
Leadership and of Your Life

Longevity has its place. But I'm not concerned about that now. I just want to do God's will. And He's allowed me to go up to the mountain. And I've looked over. And I've seen the Promised Land. I may not get there with you. But I want you to know tonight, that we, as a people, will get to the promised land!

—Dr. Martin Luther King, Jr.

When Dr. King spoke these words on April 3, 1968 at the Mason Temple in Memphis, Tennessee, he didn't know that he would be murdered in cold blood the very next day. There had been threats; thus, many believe his words show that he foresaw his death, but he still ended his speech on a positive note. Like Moses, King was prepared to die, and he faced death with no fear. He had seen a vision of what he'd been working towards, and even when the vision did not include himself, it still filled him with joy. This is the crux of transformational leadership:

- Leadership that includes sacrifice
- Leadership that does not focus on personal gain
- Leadership that grooms others for the fight to come, so that progress continues without the original leader, and in fact expands exponentially to places he couldn't reach on his own

The ultimate leader is one who is willing to develop their people so that they surpass themselves in ability, knowledge, and influence.

—*Fred Allen*

Transactional vs. Transformational Leadership

Transactional leadership is leadership by rewards and punishments. Its purpose is to maintain the status quo. Transformational leadership is leadership by consensus, based on shared values. Its purpose is to institute change—that is, growth. When we are working towards a common cause, others will take up the baton when we have run our race. The finish line may be crossed by only one, but we all share the victory.

- We are pursuing **growth** in our lives and in our work, not more of the same-old-same-old.

- We **transform** ourselves, our colleagues, our workplaces, and our communities.

In my corporate life, when I saw that I wasn't going to the mountaintop, I decided I would help others get promoted, people who shared my values and my vision for a new kind of leadership and a new kind of workplace. Over time, the culture of the company would shift toward our vision. Over time, the values of inclusiveness and diversity would prevail. I find incredible joy in this prospect of growth and transformation. I leave something behind that is worthwhile and important. I have given my all and left the world a better place.

Generational Leadership

Sometimes, the transfer of leadership from one generation to the next goes smoothly. In the story of Moses and Joshua, Moses is the one who approaches God and asks Him to appoint a clear successor. He wanted the transition of leadership to happen without strife. He understood it wasn't about him.

We can't always count on this smooth transition. When I was in college, I came home for spring break. My stepfather and mother got into a terrible fight. I went to be with her in the bedroom, while he ranted and raved outside the door. I grabbed a pistol.

"If you come in here, I'm going to use it," I shouted at him.

He didn't come in.

I didn't have to use it.

To this day, I don't like guns, because I know that if he had come through that door, I'd have used that pistol. To this day, I remember the lesson I learned: there is a point at which you must take control, you must lead. It is a leap of faith. Only when you take control can you move on. That day, the power shifted. It transferred from my stepfather to myself. It wasn't smooth, but it was necessary. Sometimes, the situation is not ideal, but the end result is achieved.

We don't get a rehearsal for life.
We have to do the best we can in the moment.

We must look at the generations before us and after us not as threats, but as the natural progression of change. There is a time one must step up and take the reins from the previous generation. After this event, my stepfather and I came to an understanding. I always loved him, and he knew that. He always loved me, and I knew that. The shift in power from one generation to the next can happen many different ways, but when the end result is change for the better, everyone benefits.

Bringing Transformational Leadership to Your Life's Purpose

Whatever your purpose in life, you can't achieve it alone. As you work toward your goals, you will be led, you will lead others, and you will have people to walk beside you. In order to make the most of transformational leadership, you can't be jealous of what others bring to the table. On the contrary, you celebrate it. Everyone is on their own path, so their purpose is different than yours, their path is different, and their destination is different.

In and of ourselves, we can only do so much, but when we empower others, we can use their diverse talents and strengths and share with one another. We then are able to benefit the company, the team, each other, and ourselves. No matter how engaging our personality might be, we still must work through others. No one has it all to themselves. We must tap the resources of others, be receptive to each other. Imagine things together. See a vision together. Get to the mountaintop together.

The act of empowering others changes lives. It is a win-win situation, for you and for the people you empower.
—William Wollcott

You and the people you empower will benefit. You work through others. You're influencing not only them, but also all the people they influence. Share the workload. Let them represent you. They are an extension of you.

In order to empower others, you must:

- …have a relationship with them. No one will follow you unless they know that you care about them. In order to care about a person, you must know them. In order to know them, you must listen to them. You must take their point of view into consideration. Relationships, of course, go two ways. So you must also let them know you. Transformational leadership does not allow you to hold yourself above others, aloof and alone. The community you create is one of relationships in all directions. When you value people and your relationship with them, this sets the foundation for influence.

- ...respect them. To inspire people to want to follow where you lead, you must show them respect. Respect, like relationships, goes both ways. If you don't respect people, they won't respect you. You need to respect people even if they may not yet always deserve your respect.

Every man is entitled to be valued by his or her best moments.
—*Ralph Waldo Emerson*

No person is perfect. You must respect not only their success, but also their failure. Remember, failure is the first step to success. If we don't respect failure, then we aren't being true to our belief that it's better to have tried and failed than not to have tried at all. You must look to the positive in everything and everyone.

People will often seek the help to change on their own, but it may take time. We say, they came to themselves. In the Bible, Jesus tells the story of the prodigal son. Of two brothers, one takes his inheritance early. He wasted his inheritance and found himself broke, working on a pig farm. He had failed, having no money or food to eat. He came to himself when he put the pig's food to his mouth. He realized that his father's servants ate better than this, and he made his way back home filled with shame. But his father received him with joy and celebration. When the other son is angry at this reception of his brother, the father says, "You are ever with me, and all that I have is yours, but thy younger brother was lost and now he is found." It is a story of redemption and forgiveness. It is a story of how we will all fail, but if failure is met with love, there can be growth.

Modeling respect shows others how to show respect. You nurture the culture that you wish to create. You do it. Others watch. Then others take up your lead. Just like the golden rule says in the Bible. "Do unto others as you would have them do unto you."

- …be committed to them. Before you ask people to be committed to your purpose, they first must know that you're committed to it. Then, they must know that you're committed to them. You prioritize them and the purpose, and that shows you care about both. People must believe a task is worthwhile if they're going to be committed to it.
- Show people that you are 100 percent by your actions, and they will follow 100 percent with their actions. People do what people see. So you must model your behavior for them, show them how to act, and they will act accordingly. What you study is what you become.

Commitment is an act, not a word.
—*John-Paul Sartre*

- …evaluate them. What are their strengths? What are their weaknesses? What can they bring to the table? What can you do to improve their skills and outcomes? When you know what each person can and cannot do, then you can trust them to handle projects with confidence. You will bring out the best in them, and that will lead to more trust both in themselves and in you.

- ...give them permission to succeed. Make people believe they can succeed, and they will. Once people recognize that you are committed to helping them, they will believe in themselves, too. They will then be able to succeed on their own. You must release them into their own success. Let them soar and let them know that you're watching their flight with pride and joy. If they feel you clinging to them or holding them back, the dynamic for change will be stilted. Letting go is a moment of trust for both the leader and those he or she has led.

When to Pass on Leadership

There have been times I found myself at a bedside in the hospital beside a person at the end of their lives. I tell them, I'm going to pray for you. Let's give God some reasons why you should get out of this bed. This leads them to think about what they still need to finish. What they still have to accomplish. What work they still have to do.

If they could come up with these things, I would encourage them: You need to get well to do these things. Keep pushing. Get to that place. What propels you is the why: I still have something to do.

But sometimes, people would tell me, I'm tired. I don't feel like going on any further. People sense when their journey is done, like my oldest sister who passed away. Just before she passed away that last Christmas holiday season, she went out of her way to give and give to others, food and gifts, time and love. She was finalizing things, saying goodbye. She was completed.

Leadership, like life, has a limit. We watch the signs and see when it's time to step aside and when to forge forward. We sense it. Like Moses, we say, I've been to the top of the mountain, and now I'm on the way back down with a message from God. We pass on the message and the love, even if we ourselves will not reach the end of the journey together.

CONCLUSION

You can't spike the football on the five-yard line.

How to Know When Your Journey is Complete

Now that you've read this book, you've come to understand that you have a purpose in life. You know now that you must:

- Educate yourself to gain the knowledge you need to achieve your purpose.
- Make a plan for action toward your purpose. If the mind can perceive it, you can achieve it.
- Take the leap of faith necessary to begin moving toward your purpose.
- Endure and persevere through the hardships that are sure to come.
- You have also come to understand that even these four steps are not enough to achieve your purpose, because no one can achieve their purpose alone. You need to bring others along on your journey. You must now apply these four steps needed to achieve your purpose toward incorporating transformational leadership into your journey:

- Educate yourself on the kinds of leadership available to you and when they are the correct choice.
- Make a leadership plan for action on how you will attract people: who will mentor you, whom you will mentor, and who will walk beside you.
- Take the leap of faith to accept that you must be a leader. Believe that you must engage others, and that no goal can be met alone. No matter where you are on your journey, you have something to give others, and others have something to give you. Accept these people in your life. Look out for them. Bring them in.
- Endure and persevere through the tests of leadership. Know that there will be failures, and accept them as opportunities to learn and move forward.

Now, it is time to act. Reading this book is the beginning. Going out into the world and acting on these words is the next step. Let's start by being intentional with a game plan.

The last step is knowing when your journey is done. How do you know when to stop? How do you know that you are in the place where you are meant to be?

Never.

Never, ever stop.

No matter how much you accomplish for yourself, there will always be others looking up to you, reaching out to you, and pushing you further. This isn't a negative. This is what will continue to bring you everlasting joy.

You owe it to yourself to keep on moving. Keep on growing. Do more than you ever thought possible, and then do some more after that. Dream as if you'll live forever. When you're working toward your purpose and working out of love for others, you'll never tire. You'll find joy in everything you do. You won't wilt away like a flower. You will blaze away into the life thereafter while leaving a positive legacy behind for others to follow.

It's not the end that's hard, because there is no end. Your life's work is just that: the work of a lifetime.

It's the beginning that's hard.
Taking that first step.

You've got this. You might be afraid. You might not have faith in yourself. But if you don't pursue your purpose, you will be filled with regret.

I challenge you to take that step.

You're not alone. You are uniquely qualified for your own personal journey. No need to be jealous or envious of anyone.

Look around you. Everyone is on a journey. Everyone has a purpose.

Keep a positive outlook, welcome others into your life, and you can achieve anything.

Keep moving forward, and the journey will contain its own rewards.

Never, ever give up.

Never, ever stop.

In your work, life, and community, you can become the person you were meant to be. I believe in you. But what's more important: do you believe in yourself?

ABOUT THE AUTHOR

DR. CHARLES REDD
LEADERSHIP MOTIVATOR

With his expertise in building teams, inspiring excellence and generating results, Dr. Charles Redd and his team have captured the perfect way to bring each of his assets and a bright new persona to the marketplace in his timely new podcast, Dr. Charles Speaks. In this fresh, new podcast, "Dr. Charles" delivers encouraging teachings and nuggets from his heart and career. He shares his profound, yet practical approaches to developing successful leaders and owning trailblazing careers. Each podcast is thought-provoking and they are adding followers on every major podcast platform including iTunes, iHeart Radio, Google Play Music, Spotify, Stitcher, YouTube, and more as listeners get motivated with Dr. Charles.

Dr. Charles Redd possesses a Doctorate of Ministry in Transformational Leadership; Masters in Religious Studies; Master's Degree in Management & Supervision; and a Bachelor's of Science Degree in Communications and Business Administration. He is a Certified John Maxwell Member, recognized as a Mentor, Teacher, Trainer and Speaker.

Dr. Charles Redd can be an asset to your ministry, business, or leadership team. To discuss how Dr. Charles can empower your organization contact us today.

WWW.DRCHARLESREDD.COM
@DRCHARLESREDD

StoryTerrace